Susan
You ARE
UNStoppable.
Stacey

OWN YOUR OWN

SHIft

The Passion, Power & Freedom to
Be **UNSTOPPABLE**

STACEY RUTH

Copyright © 2020 by Stacey Ruth.

All rights reserved. No part of this publication may be reproduced, distributed, or transmitted in any form or by any means, including pho-tocopying, recording, or other electronic or mechanical methods, without the prior written permission of the publisher, except in the case of brief quotations embodied in critical reviews and certain other noncommer-cial uses permitted by copyright law. For permission requests, write to the publisher, addressed "Attention: Permissions Coordinator," at the email address below.

Stacey Ruth
hello@staceyruthsays.com
www.staceyruthsays.com

Book Layout by Darlene Carter
Book Cover Design by Elise Reid
Book Editing by Kris Firth

Ordering Information:
Quantity sales. Special discounts are available on quantity purchases by corporations, associations, and others. For details, contact the "Special Sales Department" at the email address above.

Own Your Own Shift/Stacey Ruth.—1st edition
ISBN: 978-0-9995156-3-1

CONTENTS

I have tremendous gratitude for the insightful women who took ownership of their own shift as a part of the making of this book: Kathryn Crawford, Stephanie Myers, Lorri Palko, Elise Reid and Susie Weatherly — you make me better.

Dedicated to Umat Kamam:
You are my inner fire.

The question isn't who is going to let me;
it's who is going to stop me.
—AYN RAND

WHAT WE THINK, WE ARE

It was 1996. I had left my husband, Mark, standing back at the parking lot with the other tourists who had come to take a few photos but weren't willing to hike up to the vortex at the Sedona Airport Mesa. Although he was a self-proclaimed adrenaline junkie, Mark adamantly refused to make the climb. "I'm a skydiver who is afraid of heights," he loved to tell people.

I, however, was not afraid of heights. I headed up. The energy in the place had pulled me in from the moment we arrived in the Red Rock Valley. I had never felt anything like it, and I was buzzing with an energy of my own I could not begin to describe.

Mark and I had been married six years, and for the last five of those, neither of us had stopped working at our respective jobs. Typically, we fell out of bed at 5:00 AM, were at work by 7:00 AM, ate lunches at our desks most days, came home by 7:00 or 8:00 PM, had a late dinner, and repeated the routine again, working many weekends and occasional all-nighters, without ever taking vacation.

I was a twenty-eight-year-old art director, and he was a thirty-three-year-old engineer. We each made reasonable salaries at global companies, but we never seemed to save very much, even with our excessive work schedules. It was nothing short of a miracle that we had managed to bring ourselves here to Sedona for five days as a result of a recommendation from a friend.

So here I was: atop the Airport vortex. Alone, except for a couple of strangers, sitting in their own bubbles of meditation. My back was to my husband, and my face was towards the endless view of the red rocks, pulsing with light and energy. A hawk was looping slowly over the valley, and, as the October breeze brushed my face, I sat down at a respectful distance from my new companions, just to soak in the view and to make the climb worthwhile.

What I felt, for the first time in at least five years, and perhaps most of my twenty-eight, was pure, uninterrupted silence. I could feel it physically, both inside and outside of myself. It was enormous, expanding out into infinity. The silence churned in my stomach and my solar plexus, pulsing out in all directions, while the silence of the valley pulsed forward to meet it. I truly believe that in my wonder, for the briefest flash of time, I stopped thinking.

I was. Here. Now.

In that place, time stopped for me. Then, simultaneously, I heard a voice inside my head. It formed a very quiet, neutral, clear, and powerful sentence: "It is time to go out on your own."

What I interpreted the voice to mean was that I was ready to leave my current job and start my own business. (Today, I suspect it also referenced my marriage to Mark as well.)

The voice came from out of the silence, and disappeared again. I have never attributed it to a deity, or anything other than my own inner voice. But it filled me with the chill of otherworldly recognition nonetheless. I had touched the infinite, which left its enormous, indelible fingerprints across my being for the rest of my life, even when I drifted into a forgetfulness that lasted decades.

All the silent expansion rushed back into me, like a genie returning into its bottle, and I headed back down to where Mark was waiting for me as the sun was setting into deep purple shadows that stretched across the road, disappearing into the desert.

I was excited beyond words and barely able to stay inside my own skin.

That day set the wheels in motion towards starting my first agency, the WOW Factory, which launched sixty days later, with two substantial clients already in place. It also coincided with the beginning of the end of my marriage with Mark a year later. The two ideas were intertwined for me, since he never got completely comfortable with the risk I was taking to leap into the entrepreneurial unknown. My rapid shift came without warning, on what seemed to him to be nothing more than a whim.

In an instant I had changed how I thought about myself entirely. Instead of seeing myself as a victim of my circumstances, just accepting whatever life handed me, I stepped into an active role of creating a life I truly wanted. I had quietly dreamed of being a creative, powerful businesswoman, believing it was never going to happen.

I wanted it, but I had been told that was absurd, and I believed what I had been told. Even so, I had spent years of my fantasy life imagining vividly, in great detail, what it would feel like and look like—right down to the clothes I would be wearing and the food I would eat. That day in October I took a bold step towards my vision.

It was also the day every aspect of my thinking came fully into play. My conscious and subconscious worked together precisely as the mind is meant to function in its highest and most unlimited form. It took me another twenty years before I really understood what that actually means. What had happened was that all that daydreaming work had actually been extremely powerful and productive. I had not consciously realized how my belief about what I could and couldn't do had been holding me back and strangling my creativity.

I had cultivated a powerful vision for what I wanted that I had nurtured for years in vivid detail—never telling anyone, but repeatedly diving into it, and building it over time. My belief system that said I couldn't, shouldn't, and wouldn't ever be more literally crumbled under the pressure the vision had accumulated. My vision I had built so beautifully and so consistently then came bursting through.

The mind is still a barely charted mystery, where thoughts and beliefs are our constant, sometimes invisible, companions. They churn endlessly. In our dreams, thoughts flow like a liquid, unbound by any physical law, taking the form of symbols and metaphors, shifting and sweeping us along as we observe. Then, while we are awake, it appears that we actively retake the reins, maintaining control of our focus and mental activity.

Whether these mental trains form inspired ideas or get lost in the fog of fear and worry, they are unceasing. It is our shared, universal experience. However, our thoughts are not always as conscious as we might like to think.

In our waking life, 90 percent of our decisions are made from an emotional and subconscious realm—the dream world is not so far away as we might imagine.

There is a pattern and an order behind our thoughts—even

those in dreams—that may not be obvious at first. When we understand it, we gain mastery of our personal experience that can seem almost miraculous.

Underneath our thinking and behind the shroud of our feelings, there lies a set of fundamental beliefs. These are beliefs we have collected about ourselves, the world, and our relationship to the world. When we can uncover these beliefs—many of which are hidden even from ourselves—we can master our own success with predictable precision.

We operate simultaneously in the conscious and the subconscious plane. In business, for example, we may consciously acknowledge the need for the income represented by more or better clients, while subconsciously we may be afraid of the work these new clients will demand of us since we are already operating at full capacity. The two ideas—conscious and unconscious—are at odds with one another.

We may also be afraid that any marketing promotion we do will fall flat or end in rejection, so we default to inaction. These fears are feelings based on beliefs we are barely aware of, and, depending on their strength and how subtly they insinuate themselves into our thought patterns without interruption, they frame our reality.

Then there are the times we suffer from exhaustion and overwhelm—tortured by endless deadlines, navigating family demands, and unable to keep up with our finances, get to meetings on time, or pick up the kids from daycare before it closes. Just forget about taking a weekend off, desperately wanting relief and support!

Yet, at the same time, when anyone suggests we might get outside support, we hold a subtle belief that we must control every aspect of our lives. So, we have a story that the right help is just not available or affordable, or it takes longer to hand off than to just do it ourselves. We may even go through the motions of looking for helpers and engaging them, only to be even more frustrated and disappointed when our new hires underwhelm us.

We get to feel like victims of circumstances as a result, and so we stay on the same track as before. We prove the very thing we believe by choosing it over and over again. That's just one sort of story—one that was definitely mine, and that of many other entrepreneurs I know. Still, it isn't the only sort of story we might tell ourselves.

It is important to note that some of our beliefs and our stories are formed as a result of painful and terrifying experiences. This creates trauma. If I am describing you, then be aware that you may need specialized, professional help to compassionately reintegrate your whole self. You may still gain a tremendous amount out of this book and even experience some success with what it offers, but your primary task is to help yourself heal those gaping wounds before you can truly move forward.

Know that no matter what your story is, it doesn't have to be this way. You can literally change your mind. You can change your thinking. You can dig into the obscure world of your deeply held beliefs and change the ones that no longer serve you. This is where it all must begin. It doesn't happen because of a new client, or a day off, or the right diet—because those things are just addressing the symptom until you change your thinking.

Everything we undertake begins with an idea. From birth until death, we are forever conceiving, choosing, and acting on an idea. In fact, we make approximately 35,000 decisions every single day. If we cannot grasp the unspeakable power of our thoughts to either free us or to hold us prisoner, then not much else in our experience will make much sense.

Our thoughts, though invisible to us, are more powerful than any tangible, external circumstance. It was only through my intense excitement and allegiance to the idea of starting my own business that I moved rapidly and seamlessly to put everything into place to begin my business in just days—in spite of having no savings, no equipment or software, only the smallest amount of support (and a great deal of negativity and fear) from my husband, tremendous resistance in my current workplace as they tried to convince me to stay, and my own doubt about my worthiness and abilities. My vision carried me past my circumstances, which is a testament to the force of vision and intention to shift old beliefs.

Thoughts can also easily form into quicksand that pulls us into a prison of our own thinking. We are just as capable of falling into a repeating pattern of choosing and acting out the same experience over and over again, developing a belief about the experience we are having. There is an actual physical "groove" that is created in our brain as a result of repetitive thought. The more we think it, the more we are likely to keep thinking it, and we even look for reinforcement and validation for it.

When we have an intensely positive experience, like landing a big project in our business, or falling in love, we have a thought about the experience, such as, "This is the kind of project I am capable of winning now," or "This is my soul mate!"

These thoughts inform our beliefs (assuming there are no other more deeply ingrained beliefs to combat them), and we now have a belief that big projects and intense love are our new reality. If we are successful in creating a belief around this, we will actively seek evidence to support it, largely by pursuing and acting in alignment with what we know it takes to win more big projects or nurture a loving relationship.

However, if we have had an intensely negative experience, such as an extended period of debt, it can feel like a tremendous failure. If we then think of ourselves as a failure, we can start to build a deeply negative belief around that thought. We begin to look for other examples of proof that this belief about ourselves being a failure is valid. It becomes the proverbial self-fulfilling prophecy and a loop that continuously feeds itself by seeking to prove itself over and over.

There are three common ways out of this loop, each of which can cause our thinking to jump the tracks entirely. These are ways that, when we are ready, can simply redirect us.

The first way to exchange an old idea for a new one is through tremendous pain. Pain is often required to shake us out of an idea we have been holding onto. It can be emotional pain or it can be physical pain, but pain will override a habitual thought if it is intense enough. A foundational concept behind the Twelve Steps of Recovery is that alcoholics and addicts must "hit a bottom" (be in serious pain) in order to want to think differently about themselves and their addictions. For the rest of us, it means thinking differently about our self-imposed limitations and ineffective choices.

The pain of hitting a bottom leads to what is called surrender. Surrendering an old idea can be one of the most difficult things any of us ever do, so pain serves as a wake-up call I refer to as the "cosmic two-by-four." It breaks through the illusion that an ineffective approach is actually helping us. It transforms the fears of failure, disappointing others, not having enough money, time, or work—and turns them into nonissues in comparison to the pain. The pain must be enough to command all your attention. We stop resisting change, because the pain is bigger than our resistance.

Pain is like flipping on the lights so we can see that our thinking is actually severely damaging to us. A painful bottom isn't pretty.

It shows up as nervous breakdown, exhaustion, identity theft, lawsuits, hospitalization, incarceration, homelessness, divorce, bankruptcy, or serious illness to name a few. Although these things are possible without being associated with this transformative bottom, when they are, it is impossible to miss.

My vortex experience came hard on the heels of a lengthy period of exhaustion. I had depleted my physical and emotional reserves with a self-imposed, five-year career death march. The stress had been unmanageable, leaving me curled up in the fetal position in tears that I could never explain. It was also not surprising that Mark and I were in couples' therapy, since the romance had left our relationship, unable to compete with our work lives. I was miserable, ripe with pain.

Five days of freedom from that dull and brutal routine had been enough to open my eyes, at least temporarily, to a new idea—an expansive idea. I jumped the groove in my brain. I was temporarily in both a different thought groove and belief system.

The truth is that old ideas never really go away, and old beliefs wait for us in the wings. They are familiar. They are ingrained, and that is not because we are weak or flawed. The pathway they create physically remains in our brain for the rest of our lives. Our task is to create a groove for the new idea that is deeper than the old one, through repeated practice.

Pain is, unfortunately the most common impetus for shifting from one modality of thinking to another. But it isn't the only one.

The second way to change our thinking is through impression. This is how we form our beliefs in the first place as young children. Hence the term "impressionable." Those early beliefs become the foundation of our go-to ideas. Behind every idea there is a powerful belief feeding it.

Most of these beliefs are outside of our conscious awareness, and although most were formed in our early childhood, they can crop up later as well. They can be impressed on us by our parents, our teachers, our society, and our culture. We accept them without question, although they can sometimes be thoroughly baseless and unintentionally transmitted. We choose them without recognizing that our beliefs are, in fact, always a choice.

Examples of these chosen beliefs could be that we are capable or incapable; smart or stupid; that there is always an ample supply or there is endless lack and limitation; that a particular religion is better or worse than others; a certain demographic is threatening the common good or not; that too much wealth is corrupting or the only goal worth attaining; and so on. These beliefs turn into self-affirming or self-defeating ideas. A belief that "I am incapable" quickly turns into the idea that "I shouldn't try, since I am likely to fail." A belief that a certain demographic is dangerous becomes the foundation of the idea that I must protect myself from certain individuals. Equally, a belief that I am unstoppable creates the idea that trying new things is highly desirable and likely to create something incredible.

Our beliefs are neither right nor wrong, but they either help us to grow and build a fulfilling life—or they stand between us and what we desire. Our beliefs form the framework of how we see ourselves and how we interact in the world. Without them we would be adrift and formless. However, when our lives unfold in ways that are uncomfortable, depleting, diminishing, frustrating, exhausting, painful, or frightening, beneath is a belief that is causing the discord. We find ourselves bumping up against a wall of reality and getting bruised in the process.

Interestingly, while a belief is behind every thought, we are fully capable of changing and altering our beliefs by seeding them with a new thought. It is entirely possible to shift our beliefs the exact same way we formed them—by receiving a new impression from someone else. And that impression reaches our belief system through our thoughts.

One of the most common ways to shift a belief through impression as an adult is through some sort of class study, coaching, or mentorship. Seeing someone else having an experience that we want desperately for ourselves can be all it takes to push through a limiting idea and leave it behind forever. For example, seeing someone build a sound business plan for a company that has been drifting and turn it around can provide hope that we could do the same.

Observing a before-and-after example of a workout routine that can take years of body atrophy and transform it into vitality may impress on us that we can have the same results. Working with a coach or mentor who holds our hand through a process of change, asking challenging questions and offering alternative approaches, can pierce the armor of an established idea enough to make us at least willing to entertain another, different idea.

Typically, the process of impression shifts our thinking only when ideas are not deeply ingrained and limiting beliefs are not as dear to us. This is why most often it happens while we are young and—as we say—impressionable. All "impressionable" means is that we have not formed those deep grooves in our brain yet.

The third way to change an old idea is through inspiration. This is when the voice in our head breaks through the noise of our ongoing thoughts like a lightning bolt. Rarely does inspiration hit when we are deep in a negative thought pattern. It occurs more readily when someone has already experienced some previous transformation and has practice releasing old, limiting ideas. The only way to jump to inspiration without previous transformation is what I experienced—when we have hit the pause button in our life.

When we pause, our carefully constructed defenses that preserve our ideas and beliefs are upended. There is no frame of reference. The pause is a zone of neutrality and unlimited possibility. So, when I sat down in that moment at the vortex, the voice of inspiration gushed up into my consciousness with tremendous force. Inspiration is like that. It is always seeking entrance into our conscious mind, if only our thoughts will be still enough to stop damming up the lake of inspiration that wants to flow naturally.

The realization that we can change our thoughts, instead of simply passively receiving them, is the second most powerful idea I know. The most powerful idea is that changing our thoughts actually changes our experience, not the other way around. It is the ultimate statement of personal responsibility, which single-handedly removes all excuses for settling for anything less than spectacular in any aspect of your business or your life.

SHIFT HAPPENS

People do change. In fact, we are always changing. Most of the shifts we make in our life are natural and we are able to make them with moderate or no effort. However, there are those changes that we long for, but we just can't quite seem to make the leap from "here" to "there." Even if we do change briefly, we find ourselves sucked right back into the old pattern we thought we were rid of! Those are the places our soul most needs to grow.

These stuck places are where we have long-held limiting beliefs in that brain groove. It is going to take more than wanting to make a change for us to shift. The great news is that real, sustainable shift is possible for most people by following the shift process in this book.

I have had numerous personal shift experiences like the Sedona vortex experience and have worked with many others to create their own shifts. There are common threads in them all. My studies of metaphysics, twelve-step recovery, mindfulness, neuroscience, and spiritual laws found in most major world religions have led me to a synthesis that is the foundation of this book and my transformational coaching and workshops.

I hope you enjoy this amazing journey and the exercises I am providing to guide you on your way. So, if you're ready, let's shift together!

WHY ARE YOU HERE?

WE ALL WANT to live with purpose. It is a thread that runs throughout humanity. We each have fundamental need for certainty, variety, significance, love, connection, growth, and contribution. Purpose is among these, but growing numbers of us, especially our younger generations, admit they feel they are missing a sense of purpose. There is freedom, power, and passion we activate when we know what we are meant to do. Consciously or not, we spend much of our lives searching for the inspiration and fulfillment this inner confidence promises.

However, when someone like myself comes along and asks the question, "Why are you here?" I am frequently met with a blank stare or confusion. It's like that universal dream where we show up for the test and can't remember any of the answers, and, to add to our humiliation, we aren't wearing any clothes. So let me reassure you—when it comes to finding your purpose, there is no final exam.

No one will be grading you. In fact, there are no right or wrong answers—only your answers.

In order to find answers, the most important thing is first to know the questions. When we ask better questions, we get better answers.

If you are feeling stumped considering why you are here, you are not alone. Only a few of us will succeed in finding our answer; that is, only a few of us will feel we have really found our reason to exist. Some, sadly, will conclude we can never know. Even sadder, many will determine there is no purpose to their life. That doesn't mean it's a crazy pursuit. In fact, I am confident it is the only pursuit that matters.

Nonetheless, I have not yet met the self-help guru who can deliver our individual purpose to us on a silver platter. We're going to have to get our hands dirty digging for it. I'm going to give you tools to do precisely that. Our society is not built to provide those opportunities for the individual to explore. If we want to live on purpose, we must take matters into our own hands, and claim the time and the importance for ourselves to understand it.

There's no one we can ask about our inner desires, except us. Still, we don't have much opportunity to practice this very personal conversation. From relationships to careers, and from self-worth to net worth, success has been defined for us by others; our parents, teachers, peers, organizations, marketers, political parties, and religions have all shaped the boundaries of what we are allowed to entertain as possible for ourselves. Whether we react positively or negatively to this outside guidance, we are typically reacting to them instead of following our inner guidance system.

We are taught to give more value to external validation of our truth than to internal validations. After all, who are we to know what we believe? This approach turns us wrong side out at best, and it sends us to a dark place of despair at worst.

Trying to manage our internal self-worth by controlling our external circumstance is like trying to drive on an unfamiliar road in the dark, with no headlights. There's a possibility you might navigate it, but it's exceedingly difficult, stressful, wildly unreliable, and you are likely to wind up in the ditch. Nonetheless, that's what we are trying to do much of the time.

ANSWERING THE CALL

When faced with the profound and deceptively simple question "Why are you here?" the answer is typically "I'm not really sure" or "I don't believe I have a purpose."

If this is your answer, then know that you are in good company. That was my story for decades, and I know countless others who share this temporary "purpose blindness." While it's typical to be at least a little unsure of our "why," we also feel like we are supposed to know what it is, even when we don't. A study reveals that two-thirds of us admit to feeling jealous of colleagues and friends who seem to have their entire world in order—at least on the outside. This is because we are judging our inner uncertainty—or even chaos—by the appearance of external order for others. Not only that, 80 percent of respondents indicated they felt their life lacked purpose and meaning.

Just search the internet for memes and articles about a higher purpose, calling, and sense of worth. When you do, the deluge of positivity might make you feel that if you don't have absolute clarity of purpose then you failed the universal enlightenment exam!

There are many wise-sounding, bite-size nuggets of truth floating around the consciousness of the internet, but, at the same time, there is no clear path to finding our own truth. Knowing a lot of other people feel the same way rarely makes us feel better, either. Misery might love company, but it loves not being miserable even more.

We struggle individually with understanding what purpose is, even if we attempt to go looking for it. When we do, our need for certainty is threatened right away. If you are currently lost somewhere in your quest for purpose, but are hopeful that you can find it—you can.

There is something incredible waiting for you. It is a new sense of personal freedom without limitations. There is enormous power available to you, regardless of your circumstances. There is also a real passion anyone can access, which provides the joy we crave.

If that sounds a little bit over the top, I understand. I have been where you are, and I know a lot of others who have been in situations they thought could not be overcome, such as addictions, economic hardships, and being victims of deep cultural biases. Nonetheless, countless of us have made the shift. On the other side we found real joy. That's what's waiting for you.

GOING WITH THE FLOW

Going with the flow of life—which is a default and largely unconscious approach—is not the same thing as being in the flow—where we are guided by our inner purpose and wisdom. It is entirely possible to be a success by just going with the flow. I certainly did it for years. When we do it well, going with the flow creates measurable, tangible results such as wealth, possessions, credentials, and awards. It's comfortable and we get a lot of societal affirmations for it. It can be quite seductive. In fact, most of the survey respondents I referred to earlier cited financial lack as their main obstacle to finding meaning and purpose. So, if you have the external proof of success, why change?

When we go with the flow, there's a trade-off. We turn over our happiness, our meaning, and our fulfillment to what is going on around us. We become passive recipients, and often victims, of whatever life hands us.

We marry the person just because they asked us (I actually did this), enter a particular course of study because our parents advocated for it (I did this too), or take the job because it was in front of us (yep, that's three out of three for me).

This is a risky approach, because "the flow" can just as easily turn on us. That's what happened to so many during COVID-19. Since this sort of success is external, it is also not in our control. We might think we can control our circumstances, but results are mixed at best. External circumstances have a random quality to them, even when they seem predictable and manageable on the surface. All it takes is one little pandemic to alter everything we thought we knew about reality.

Although we have the illusion of control in the day-to-day choices, our intentionality and focus is always on what's outside of us, not what's inside. We will explore this idea in great depth later, but the principle here is counter to what most of us have been taught: we only have power over our own thoughts and actions and nothing else.

When we go with the flow, we suspend our search for personal preferences. We allow our circumstances to define our thoughts, actions, beliefs, and, ultimately, us. This approach can be exhausting, disappointing, and even depressing.

I recall, at age twenty-four, lying in bed in the middle of the day, repeatedly, weeping inconsolably, with absolutely no idea why. I had been married a year. My work was meticulous, deadline-driven, and stressful. I had just graduated college and didn't have any friends in the new city where my husband and I lived.

My husband traveled for work over half the year, which left me alone much of the time. Where I had thought marriage would be my answer, instead I was isolated and adrift. My frequent meltdowns traumatized my husband, who simultaneously tried to comfort me and anxiously urged me to snap out of it.

Although I was not self-aware enough at the time to understand this, I had abandoned what I truly wanted in a relationship, regardless of what a smart, kind, funny, thoughtful person my husband was. He didn't abandon me. I did. My inner self was in very real, extreme pain.

My husband, even with his wonderful qualities, was a poor match for me. He had been interested in me, and available to me, and I had gone with the flow, without considering whether he and I were well matched in what we cared about, what we spent time on, and how we expressed affection or supported one another.

At some level I had an inkling of what was wrong. I suspected it was my choice of marriage partner, but it didn't occur to me that I ever actually had a choice. The flow had a strong undertow and it pulled me out to sea very fast. In the end, seven years later, I bailed on the marriage in a very ungracious manner, which left scars on us both.

When we turn our fulfillment over to these external factors, such as wealth and the approval of others, a funny thing happens: enough is never enough. At the University of Buffalo, researcher Lora Park and her colleagues investigated the impact when self-worth becomes tied to financial success. Those who did make the financial/worth connection engaged in more social comparisons, experienced more stress and anxiety, and felt less autonomy than those who didn't tie their self-worth to income, regardless of their actual economic status.

So, although most of us are just going with the flow, and some of us are doing it with relatively positive results, it still leaves us with a certain sense of discontentment. This discontentment can be subtle, like the desire for more of what we already have to excess. It can also be profound, like the vague depression more than three hundred million of us report suffering worldwide. That's the same depression I experienced during my meltdowns.

WHY OUR "WHY" MATTERS

If we don't believe our purpose is vital—and that our lives actually depend on knowing our purpose—we will not pursue it. When we treat it casually, then it is only a very nice idea, and we can look at it next year. Unfortunately, that's what too many of us do.

So let's look at our present reality. At the publishing of this book, there are more than five million new businesses started every year. These businesses are not only an enormous influence on our economies and our culture; they also are one of the main sources of our self-worth. This is true whether we own the company or whether we are employees there.

Our businesses are a reflection of the personalities, values, and purpose of the individuals who comprise them. Yet, for just a handful of decades, we have established a pervasive mindset that business is separate from our personal lives and our individuality. We have treated emotion and intuition and instinct as the enemy of success in the business arena. This shows up in how we talk about work and life balance as if they are somehow separate.

This would all make perfect sense if it were working. Yet it isn't. Of the more than five million businesses started every year, 90 percent close in the first year. Ninety-four percent of American workers are experiencing work-related stress, and that stress is translating into absenteeism, attrition, and chronic, stress-related disease.

All of this is happening in a global society that is noticeably purpose-deficient at the individual level. It is precisely this reason that we drift and experience all the stress, anxieties, related illnesses, high dissatisfaction, and low self-worth. Lack of purpose is, quite literally, killing us. It is killing people, businesses, society, and our world.

The answer is to seek and capture our individual purpose not only as if our very lives depended on it, but as if every other life depended on us finding it as well. When one person finds their purpose, they catch fire. That fire lights the way for others, and it is not only the antidote for what ails us, it is as contagious as the disease of purposelessness that has infected us for far too long.

WHAT OUR "WHY" IS NOT

There are a number of myths many of us have about our individual purpose. These myths form a barrier between us and our "why." We get stuck in them, and can't find our footing.

The first myth is that we each have just one purpose. As a result, when it isn't immediately obvious, we assume either it doesn't exist or we are deeply flawed for not seeing it. For the rest of this book, when we refer to purpose, it will be a catchall word for any and all of the motivations that give our lives meaning.

As an example, my roles of coach, author, speaker, minister, marketer, wife, daughter, stepmother, grandmother, animal lover, world traveler, and fire starter are all perfectly valid channels for my purpose. I do not need to be just one thing or do just one thing to fulfill my purpose. Each of these roles—and many, many more—combine to fulfill my purpose of helping businesses and their leaders become conscious of their purpose.

Within these roles, I receive wonderful insights and opportunity to practice the one thing my purpose must have: a whole, authentic me. I also am fulfilling the purpose of learning to love, helping others heal from their old wounds, and creating a better world. It all matters. Every experience, relationship, skill, and interest matters. So don't get bogged down in the myth that your purpose must be one thing, and one thing only.

The second myth is that our purpose must be enormous and world changing. We are all world changers, but only occasionally can we know precisely how we make a difference. I was personally reminded of this on a twelve-step recovery weekend retreat.

I took a walk beside the lake with an Indian woman, and as we discussed our journeys to finding this spiritual practice, she shared with me that I was the reason she was there. As it turns out, she was in the audience when I spoke to a small group in a treatment center about the fundamentals of recovery two years prior to our stroll together. Her husband was the one in treatment, and although she pursued the twelve steps from that day forward, he did not.

Ultimately he died from complications of his disease.

My friend didn't stop there. She explained that after his death she returned to India for a short while and found one small meeting in the provincial town where she was staying. They had one woman who led the meeting every time and who translated literature into the local dialect for the group, to the best of her ability, out of what little they had. Unfortunately, her translation from English was highly inaccurate.

My new friend shared how she translated several pieces of literature more accurately and now sponsors a couple of those women still living in India. There's new hope for recovery somewhere in India because I spoke one time at a treatment center, and thought very little of it.

Our impact might not ever be fully clear to us or anyone else. Nevertheless, we all matter, whether we do it intentionally, ever recognize it, or not. It is woven into our existence. For this very reason it is necessary to understand that our purpose does not have to be grandiose.

Most of the major religions refer to humanity as a light in the world. Whether you subscribe to this idea that you are born to be inherently, vitally important, let me assure you that this book will not ask you to be anything other than you already naturally are. In order to live into your purpose, the one thing you must be is you.

The third myth is that your purpose is absolute. My purpose during my twenties is not remotely my purpose today, nor could I possibly have embraced my current purpose in my fifties when I was in my twenties. I didn't have enough personal life experience. My purpose has grown, morphed, and expanded as I have evolved.

In my twenties and thirties my purpose was to help others visually communicate with greater clarity.

Today my purpose is to help others understand who they really are with greater clarity.

My purpose has evolved.

Because our purpose often does evolve and shift, it is vitally important that we check in with ourselves regularly to see whether we are still "on purpose" once we are clear what our purpose truly is.

There certainly are common threads that have run throughout our lives that provide clues to our purpose. My strong desire to write showed up even in my early childhood, as did my love of experiences beyond the five senses. The clues to what you are here to do are everywhere, if and when you know to look for them.

The fourth myth is that purpose is about something outside of us. Living, as we do, in a culture that teaches us to look outside ourselves for direction and validation, it is no wonder we think our purpose is somewhere outside of us as well. Many individuals who claim to be aware of their purpose, when pressed, will say it is to ensure a better life for their kids, run their own company one day, or retire by age fifty-five. There is absolutely nothing wrong with any of these goals; however, they are goals, not a purpose.

There are a number of definitions of what a personal purpose actually is, but most agree on this: A personal purpose defines who you are, not what you achieve. It reflects your passions and values. As a result, it provides clarity as you set goals of what it is you want to do. Your purpose is what guides how you want your life's story to go.

Your purpose is why you are here. Not just on this planet. Not just in this lifetime. Your purpose is why you are here, with me, reading this book, right now, about how you can own your own shift.

How can I be so certain? Because this book is about empowering you to make a meaningful shift for yourself. If you weren't stuck in some way, you wouldn't need what is on offer here. You are experiencing resistance—and that, my friend, is your purpose at work on you—whether you know your purpose right now or not.

Wherever we experience the most resistance, either internal or external, to a shift we want to make, that is where we have the greatest growth opportunity. We all are growing and healing or we wouldn't have the awareness that we want to change. I call this our "soul work," and the greater the resistance, the more it strengthens us to fulfill our purpose. The greater the resistance, the more we can learn from it.

So, when we just cannot seem to shift, it is time to pay attention. When I say, "Pay attention," I don't mean in order to blame, shame, or judge ourselves, but to simply focus on that area of our life and become curious about it. Where we focus—not where we try to force change—is where we flourish.

It is actually not necessary for you to identify your purpose to do the work in this book. In fact, it is highly likely that you may discover it at some point through this process. However, I strongly suggest that you complete the following exercises to get the wheels turning.

EXERCISES TO DISCOVER YOUR PURPOSE

Exercise 1: Find Your Core Personal Values

Values are the principles you live by, they are the foundation of our purpose. We rarely stop and consider them. When we do, we tend to go to default values we think we are "supposed" to have, like love, truth, family, compassion, etc. Those are all wonderful values, and most of us have them in a greater or lesser degree. But they may only be on the periphery of our main value system, which is uniquely ours. For instance, perhaps you value adventure, freedom, and creativity much more than truth or authenticity. Allow that to be okay. Your values are yours, and no one else's. It doesn't make you deficient, bad, or wrong. How boring it would be if we all had exactly the same values!

It's important to check in with yourself on your values; look at where you really spend your time and set your priorities. There are patterns in your daily activities that will give you clues about what you really value. If you have a nagging suspicion that the amount of time you spend at work is not really driven by your values, but rather by your fear or commitments, then allow that to be possible.

To explore your values, you can find a list of three hundred values on my website at StaceyRuthSays.com/Resources that you can download and use. Start with selecting twelve values that resonate for you, then narrow that list down to six, and finally, see if you can narrow even further to between three and four. That way you can begin to focus on how you are really living into your values every day. Begin journaling—are there areas in your life where you might be blocking yourself from being in alignment with those values? And know it is okay during this process to change your mind. After all, how much have you previously focused on your personal values up till now? This is a process of self-discovery as well as self-mastery.

Exercise 2: Get Clear About Your Passions

You read that right. Passions is plural here, because we typically have many passions. Not only that, passion and purpose are distinct, although not everyone knows this. Passion is about emotions that drive us. Our passion inspires us and is built on what makes us feel good. Purpose is the reason, or the why behind what we do, primarily as a contribution to the world.

Finding your passions is really just about what lights you up and gives you joy—or at least a deep sense of satisfaction. It does not need to be what you do to earn income—although it can be. For instance, I am passionate about hiking the many trails around our home, and I have a dream of hiking the Camino del Santiago. But I do not intend to become a travel blogger. Another passion I have is animal rights and promoting the ethical treatment of animals. I happen to believe how we treat animals directly affects how we treat one another. However, again, I am not planning to become a paid activist or a veterinarian.

Passions tend to be the places where you lose your sense of time passing, or you daydream about doing more of it. Passions are where you are compelled to show up, engage, and nurture something. Often, however, we amputate ourselves from our passions at some point, because we felt (or someone told us) they were foolish or unrealistic, or that they interfered with what was really important. If this feels like it might be your story, spend some time journaling about what you loved to do as a child, regardless of how the inner critic might try to interfere in the same voice that told us it was foolish or unrealistic. If you loved chasing fireflies, put it down. You don't have to make sense of it. Just acknowledge it. And perhaps go chase some fireflies tonight (just be sure to give them air to breathe).

Exercise 3: Make a List of Your Talents

We all have them. You might be exceptional at talking on the phone for hours—so write down "friendly conversation." You might be wildly gifted at ordering takeout, so add "creative food sourcing." My point is only this: don't be lured by the "I don't have many talents" excuse to not look for them. In other words, give yourself credit for whatever you can do easily and almost effortlessly, rather than dismissing or diminishing yourself.

Also, if all your talents seem to group around one area, such as work, challenge yourself to broaden your search. What are your talents with friends, family, in your home, self- care, personal development, etc.? Generosity is a talent. So is daydreaming. Give credit wherever it is due.

Exercise 4: Gently Look at Your Challenges

Very few lists about purpose dare discuss the idea of looking at our yucky stuff, but this is one of the main areas that shape our purpose. As the famous Rumi quote tells us, "The broken places are where the light gets in."

I suggested gently looking, because the majority of us

are harder on ourselves than anyone else, and this is not a ready-made opportunity to beat ourselves up over lost love, debt, addiction, poor job performance, or poor health. Rather, looking at your areas of challenge means looking at the places where you have the greatest channel for personal growth and healing.

Many of us, as we navigate our challenges, find them to be the most powerful drivers of our purpose, giving us inspiration to take our hard-won lessons and share them with others who are where we once were. So, as you look (don't stare) at your personal challenges—it is okay to acknowledge that they can be quite intense (like abuse, addiction, and witnessing another person's trauma), but you don't have to relive them. If you do need professional help to address them, by all means do so. Not doing so is likely one of the greatest obstacles to living a life of purpose.

Our areas of challenge also provide us with some of the most soulful understanding of the human condition. So, look. Look and ask yourself, what am I learning here? What do I know about my own strength, fears, behaviors, and beliefs that can help myself and others? This is a huge part of your story, and stories inspire us.

Exercise 5: Decide Whom You Want to Help

Purpose is never about us—it is about how we serve the larger good. The larger good can be a single individual or the entire planet. Whatever feels right to you. It can also be both. You help may come in the form of time, guidance, money, advocacy, talents, support, or presence. Yes, you can have more than one beneficiary of your gifts. All things are possible here.

Make a short list, and set it aside. Notice how you feel with each person or group you list. Does it feel empowering to think of helping them, or does it feel like a burden? The feeling is generally unrelated to the difficulty of the effort; it's more about whether you want to help out of inner passion or out of a response to perceived or actual social pressure.

Exercise 6: Write Your Epitath

No one lives forever. What would you want to be remembered for—and by whom? This can be as extravagant as you can let yourself be. Did you explore new galaxies? Did you discover a cure for world hunger? This is not the place to play small. Let the child who fantasized about what she wanted to be when she grew up come out and play.

Small is just an idea we have and a judgment we make. No, you don't have to be bold on a grand scale. If you want to be remembered as the lady who cared for all the stray cats and baked amazing brownies for the neighborhood, then more power to you. There is no judgment. One person I know who did this exercise moved from wanting to give birth to a child, which was a struggle, to adopting. The impact we have on one life can be more than we ever know.

Exercise 7: Put It All Together

Your values are your why. Your passion is the fire behind your why. Your talents are the how. The challenges are what forge your strength and wisdom. The people you help provide a channel for your energy. The impact you will have motivates your actions. Now, write down a short paragraph that captures it all.

For example, suppose you are an adventurous, free-spirited creative who was in an abusive relationship, but is extremely outgoing and an incredible cook, as well as a writer, and can lose herself in meditations and travel, but is horrible at keeping relationships out of the dumps and being anywhere on time, but loves doing thoughtful things for her friends and helping out at the local senior center. She wants to be remembered as someone who brought joy to the lives she touched and lived life to its fullest.

Her statement of purpose can look like this:

I am a creative, free, adventurous (three values) lover and nurturer of joy, who demonstrates the fullness of life to everyone I meet.

Yes, it was that simple—and also that hard. To really have self-mastery, we must embrace the good and not-so-good parts of our experience. Yes, we must embrace what we want, but that's not the end of the story. To stay there is not only a selfish action, it blocks the energy we want to experience in the first place. The objective here is to be in a place where our cup runneth over and we cannot help but share what we have received with others. First, though, we must open and receive the totality of ourselves.

CHAPTER ONE

SICK AND TIRED

ARE YOU AT THE POINT where you're sick and tired of being sick and tired? Just knowing something isn't working for you is
not always enough to make a shift. We've all been there. We find
some part of our life has become uncomfortable—or even outright
self-destructive. We sit ourselves down and have a talk. We tell our
self we are ready for a change. We might even go so far as to an-
nounce it to others.

But if simply wanting a change was all it took, we would immediately stop eating unhealthy foods and procrastinating on those
deadlines. We would leave abusive relationships and jobs without
delay. We would cast aside any addictions once and for all before
we created havoc in our own lives and the lives of those we love. If
awareness was all it took, making a shift would be so easy that entire
industries built on helping us break through, like the fitness industry,
would be out of business.

So what's stopping us? Every single day we make shifts in our lives without any assistance whatsoever. We buy clothes, homes, and cars. We get married and start families. We change jobs, learn new skills, make new friends, and grieve when someone close passes. We try new recipes, décor, and haircuts. We travel.

It isn't that these things are necessarily easy. Every shift comes with its own natural stress. It demands we leave our comfort zone of familiar behaviors to accommodate an entirely new experience. For the most part, however, we adapt to the temporary stress of these shifts, both large and small, and integrate them into our new experience. No questions asked. No weird, inexplicable internal resistance. Or, even if we do complain, as a new parent might with a sleepless infant, it doesn't stop us from doing the best we can.

This book is not designed to address these more routine shifts. Instead it looks at the places where we resist shifting—where often say we are "stuck." We can learn a lot about how we integrate routine shifts into our lives, and then apply that to the shifts we are resisting strongly. As I said in the last chapter, the shifts we resist are the places where we are most in need of healing and a soul-level transformation. This book shows, step by step, how to shed the limiting beliefs and self-imposed obstacles we build that keep us stuck, so we can live fully in our purpose. That is how we become unstoppable.

When a situation or pattern of behavior is causing us discomfort or outright harm, and we haven't been able to quickly or easily resolve it, we usually escalate to using our willpower to overcome it. This is a short-term, surface solution that does not work over the long haul. Using willpower sets up an inner conflict within us that can create a vicious cycle of disappointment and self-abuse.

Using willpower to create transformational shift is like trying to accelerate with one foot on the gas and the other foot, just as firmly, on the brake. Push the gas pedal as far to the floor as you want—when your foot is on the brake, you aren't going anywhere! Your willpower is the foot on the gas—pressing down for all you are worth. It cannot overpower whatever limiting belief your foot on the brake has in place, because it is only equally as strong—not stronger.

Not only is this stalemate frustrating, it's exhausting. Ironically, all you have to do is take your foot off the brake. Both feet are yours. You are in the driver's seat. Yet limiting beliefs are notoriously hard to see and infinitely stubborn until they are acknowledged.

Anyone who suggests that your willpower just isn't strong enough or that your awareness is not great enough to shift is likely mistaken. To begin a transformational shift you must want change so badly you would go to any length to ensure it happens—because several stages of shift that follow will demand that of you.

I'm sorry to tell you that. But if getting unstuck was that easy, you wouldn't be reading this book right now, would you? Don't give up, though—because there is a proven path out, and countless others have found it. I will be here with you every step of the way.

When you are truly sick and tired of being sick and tired, the pain of your current pattern becomes so unbearable you would do anything for a different experience—including giving up the payoff your current situation provides.

That's right. I said "payoff." A part of you is getting something out of being where you currently are. For example, as devastating as addiction can be to the addict, the substance of choice provides some relief in the moment for an extreme emotional pain. The addiction doesn't heal or cure the pain. But it numbs it for a few moments. That's a payoff.

The same could be said of being in a high-stress, abusive job. The payoff is often financial security—however nominal that security might be when compared to the pain of the situation.

In both situations, the person who feels stuck has made a choice (often unconscious) that the risk of shifting into another experience is just too great. They don't feel up to what they might have to endure—or worse, they may feel that shifting might create greater pain for them.

Transformational shift also requires you to alter your concept of who you actually are. You will need to redefine yourself. This idea of redefining ourselves is terrifying to many of us because losing our definition of who we are can feel like suicide—or worse, murder. Either way, it represents the death of who we had been.

As with any death, real or metaphorical, there is a grieving process we must undertake. We will naturally go through the seven, perfectly normal, stages of the grief process, including experiencing shock, denial, anger, bargaining, depression, testing, and—finally—acceptance.

No one I know is excited at the prospect of the exquisite discomfort grief represents. We are wired to going to extreme lengths to avoid discomfort of any kind, be it emotional or physical.

No wonder we have one foot planted firmly on the brake. Inside we are screaming, "No! Anything but this!" The greater wonder is that we make these shifts at all! What if we take our foot off the brake and we lurch forward, unable to prevent a catastrophic crash?

In real world terms, we eat the cake because we believe the craving (or the emotion behind the craving) seems too intense to bear. We say we lost our willpower, seeing a big slab of sugary goodness, and we slam our emotional foot on the brake, even though our foot on the gas would be healthier food choices and a healthier body. If we allowed ourselves to accelerate in that direction, we would have to experience the (perceived) discomfort of life without all that sugar.

Willpower won't change that belief. We didn't lose our willpower; it just isn't the right tool for what we are dealing with here.

That's what's going on inside us. However, we see lots of people who managed to bypass the cake (or whatever our version of cake is) and we compare our inner struggle to their external ease. We forget we have no idea what goes on inside them when the cake is handy. So, instead of shaming yourself for not having the willpower, give a little grace and love to the part of you that is trembling in fear. Remember, those individuals who didn't have the cake you crave either went through the process I am about to teach you or cake was never their thing anyway.

Intellectual understanding does nothing to fix this situation either. Our feelings and our beliefs are much more powerful than our conscious, rational mind. Our conscious mind owns about 10 percent of our mental real estate. The other 90 percent, filled with beliefs, emotional, nonverbal, highly intuitive processes, is far larger and stronger. You cannot overpower that sleeping Goliath with your puny logic.

Happily, people do manage to make transformational shifts, even after being stuck for long periods of time. Alcoholics and addicts attain sobriety, even in their golden years. Medically obese individuals become vibrantly healthy. We escape desperate poverty to thrive financially; overturn cruel regimes and leave dysfunctional or unfulfilling marriages; become breakout authors, politicians, and business leaders; and deliver inspiring TED talks. Wherever your purpose is taking you—whatever is driving you to push that gas pedal to the floor—you can move forward—no matter how stuck you might feel right now.

Getting unstuck requires patience and discipline, which many of my clients tell me they would like me to provide! Many of us equate those attributes with willpower. Unfortunately for these clients, patience and discipline are not actually the characteristics of willpower. Willpower is more of a sledgehammer, while patience and discipline are like the polishing of rocks by a river.

I cannot speak for anyone else, but my willpower is a surge of energy that is quickly depleted, like rocket fuel, while patience and discipline are, by their nature, sustainable and self-regenerating. They also require constant nurturing and practice.

I tell my clients I can demonstrate patience and discipline for them—but I cannot provide to them what is universally generated from within. I can show them the path, but they have to actually take the steps to experience the journey.

THE HALLWAY

The worst form of being sick and tired is a place of murky indecision, where we feel lost and directionless. This is our hallway. When we enter the hallway we are too sick and tired to go backward, but too frightened of the unknown to go forward. In other words, we are sick and tired, but not yet sick and tired of being sick and tired. We are choosing instead to stay sick and tired, or perhaps we don't know how to stop being sick and tired. Worse yet, we may understand intellectually what needs to happen, but we haven't been able to implement the practices to get unstuck.

We hang in midair. What we are doing is holding both feet down on the brake and the gas for as long as we can. This makes the hallway an exhausting, heavy, unfulfilling, dismal place to be. In short, we feel helpless and hopeless there.

Many people manage to spend months, and even years, in that

indecisive space called "the hallway." Lysbeth was one of these individuals. She would complain occasionally, "I have zero idea what I want to be doing (for a career) but I can't stand this job. I can barely make myself get up in the morning. I've never felt worse."

However, Lysbeth was strongly tethered to her lack of clarity. She even began to take antidepressants during her time in the hallway. She sounded almost proud of her acceptance of her confusing and unfulfilling situation, saying more than once, "I guess it is where I am supposed to be right now, and I have to give it the time that it takes."

Like Lysbeth, all of us have a remarkable, innate ability to rationalize any decision and any course of action (or inaction) we take. Staying in a place of inaction and indecision is a choice. It is not imposed on us from outer circumstances. On the contrary, it is our version of the deer in the headlights. Unsure what is happening, we freeze where we stand—right in the path of an oncoming vehicle.

Another analogy would be the child who manages to climb up onto the high dive but becomes incapable of either jumping into the water below, or turning around and climbing back down the ladder.

In all three cases—Lysbeth, the deer, and the would-be high diver—no one can rescue them from their situation, except them. Whether it is exploring possibilities, getting out of our own way and taking a leap of faith, returning to our previous existence, or doing more "research" on how it feels to remain stuck, the only actor is us.

The reasons we stay in the purgatory of our hallway boil down to one thing: we are afraid. The variations of that fear are:

1. We are afraid of the emotional death we call "failure," including embarrassment, disappointing others, financial loss, etc.
2. We are afraid of losing something we currently have.

3. We are afraid of not getting something we want.
4. We are afraid we are not enough.
5. We are afraid of the unknown—and the potential for even greater suffering than we are currently experiencing.

And you know what? We are right. Any and all of those things are possible. Really. They are absolutely possible. Almost every one of those fears has happened to me. I've taken the leap myself and done a face plant in proverbial concrete. I discovered there was no water in the pool when I leapt off the high dive. I've lost my income. I've not lived happily ever after with the man I thought was "the one." (Although—spoiler alert—I did eventually find him!) I've had jobs that threatened my health with their intense levels of stress and obscene disrespect.

I also have taken the leap and found myself flying instead—weightless with the incredible success of the moment. Both are possible.

The latter—flying—is actually more likely. When you leave the hallway by your own choice, you are vested in making the most of it, and, as a result, you are more likely to fly than you are to land on your face in concrete. You will at last have stopped choosing by default and stepped into a reality you are creating for yourself. At least, that's one possibility.

TWELVE STAGES OF TRANSFORMATIVE SHIFT

Here's how you can ensure you leave the hallway on your terms (the following twelve stages correspond with the numbered chapters of this book):

1. **Sick and Tired.** Know what you <u>don't</u> want. Being sick and tired of being sick and tired is actually the first stage of transformational shift. Begin with the recognition that you are missing something precious in your life. Acknowledge you are experiencing a lack of deeper meaning. Then be entirely willing to go to any lengths to fix that. We will explore how to know when you are ready.

2. **You Are Not Alone.** Know that you are not alone as you seek guidance—and before you seek answers:

    a. Learn from others who have been where you are or are headed where you want to be.

    b. Stay motivated with the masters. Study the successful individuals who inspire you. What did they do to get there?

    c. Increase your knowledge. Creating a vision for improving the world is just the first step. Next you're going to need to develop the wisdom and skill to make your dreams come true. This always begins with learning.

    d. Be open to feedback. The real trick is to avoid overconfidence. You can minimize the risk of premature action if you remain humble and be willing to adapt. Feedback is essential for progress.

    e. Get a tribe. Surround yourself with cheerleaders and like-minded supporters.

3. **Surrender.** Until we wake up to the negative beliefs we have about our chances for success, we live in a small box that limits what's possible. When we aren't getting the results we want, we change what we're doing. But if your results don't change, it's because you have a strong limiting belief that is controlling your actions. Our old way of thinking can only take us where we've already been. We must surrender much

of what we think we know. When we surrender, we find inner peace, and we begin to hear our inner guidance. Suddenly, we don't feel so lost anymore.

4. **Trust the Fire Within**. We still have fears, but we don't give them such a power over us as we used to. Our inner guidance communicates to us what needs to come next. We've not built this internal muscle much, and so we don't really trust it all that much. Therefore, it may feel scary and too big to follow the inner guidance, so we have to adjust to that idea first. We will spend some time together learning how to rely on our own guidance system more than anything else, to trust the fire within.

5. **Get Clarity.** Be clear about where you want to go. This is not a flight away from anything, but rather a pilgrimage towards something. This is where we will need our inner guidance to shed all the self-talk, doubt, inner criticism, and rejection. We will open up a channel for infinite creativity and possibility.

6. **Own Your Own Shift.** Here is where you will see the world for the first time. You know where you are headed, having shed what has held you back. You have identified the beliefs you have been holding onto, and are at least willing to begin to try a different approach with the support and guidance of others who have been where you are.

7. **Initiation.** In this stage, all patterns and conditioning that we've received from family and society come to the surface. The inner fear-based voice gets louder and stronger. The pain can reach the tolerance limits. But when we know that this is a likelihood, we also know it is temporary—coming up for us to see it at last, and release it.

8. **Plan to Practice.** Your habits determine your outcomes. Getting there requires focused action, personal discipline, and lots of energy every day to make things happen. Long-term success with your personal transformation comes down to consistency with your daily habits, repetition, time, and patience.

9. **Get Uncomfortable.** There is nothing in the world we seem to resist more than discomfort. It is encouraging to me to remember the saying, "If you are not a little bit uncomfortable, you aren't growing." Consider the intense muscle ache of doing a new workout routine or the intense pain of childbirth. Wherever your pain is on that scale, be aware that the discomfort is only temporary, and the result is nothing short of wonderful. Lean in. And lean on the trainers and midwives around you.

10. **Be the Outcome.** Human imagination is a wonderful thing that gets barely any opportunity to perform as it is meant to. We do our vision boards, littering them with pictures of people, places, and things—and this is absolutely fine for as far as it goes. It is how I found my dream home and my dream husband. However, there is something deeper required for real shift. We must immerse ourselves fully, emotionally in the experience we want to have. What will we think, feel, say, and do when we are there? Our vision must be about us, not the stuff.

11. **Choose You.** Transform your inner critic into an inner coach. Choose yourself. Research indicates that people talk to themselves about fifty thousand times a day—and that 80 percent of that self-talk is negative. At the end of the day, if you don't believe in yourself, how do you expect others to

believe in you? You need to be your biggest fan. Because if you don't value yourself to the highest degree, who will?

12. **Celebrate the Shift**. Gratitude is 100 percent necessary to retaining any shift you undertake. Appreciate your success. Failure to appreciate your shift drains confidence and returns us back into stuck faster than a bullet train. Here is where we take responsibility for the impact of our thoughts and decisions. Finally, we understand that we create our reality—and we affect the reality of those around us.

All of these twelve shift stages are necessary for transformative shift. This is true of the individual, and it is true of relationships, organizations, governments, or institutions. No stage can be effectively skipped, reordered, or given a once-over lightly.

The necessity to navigate each stage of shift is equally true of easier shifts as it is of the major, transformative shifts. The only difference is the level of fear and depth of limiting beliefs we have.

In smaller shifts, such as deciding to take a trip, we might go through the stages in less than a day—rapidly, easily, and without conscious attention. Other shifts might take weeks, months, or years for us to unpack it all. Since we do this automatically, more often than not, we haven't often stopped to consider what is involved. So, when it is time to do it consciously, we aren't sure where to begin.

Well, let me tell you, this is the place. Right where you are. So, settle in. Nothing is wrong with you. You aren't broken, and you aren't really stuck either. You knew enough about where you are to get this book. Congratulations. Now let's continue.

CHAPTER TWO

YOU ARE NOT ALONE

THE JOURNEY TO TRANSFORMATION can feel quite lonely at times. Finding guidance through this wilderness can be critical to your success.

Personally, I often prefer to be alone. I grew up as an only child in a home that was radically isolated, even in the midst of a city. In my home, we had no phone. No friends came over to play. No family visited. We didn't hang out with the neighbors. So being alone is familiar to me—just like home.

The reasons my parents chose to isolate our family unit so intensely would fill another entire book. My point in sharing this childhood isolation is that the experience defined me, shaped who I have become, and gifted me with a number of extremely useful skills, regardless of the reasons.

The first skill I learned was how to enjoy my own company. I liked myself pretty well, and I enjoyed a diverse set of highly cooperative, imaginary playmates. I could entertain myself all day and lose myself in pretend games, music, books, art, and nature.

The second skill I learned was to creatively express myself on-demand. This ability provided me with tremendous daily joy, as well as confidence in the depth of my abilities. I still love it, even to my own occasional distraction. It also provided an escape valve from the frequent intensity of my family unit. My inner world was vibrant and provided comfort, any time I wanted to withdraw there. Creativity is my safe and happy place.

The third skill I learned, perhaps ironically, was the importance of having a tribe. Perhaps because of my isolation, and perhaps just as a natural personality trait, amplified by my isolation, I became incredibly adept at making fast friends at school. I could have a best friend in just minutes, just by acting as if I had known the person all my life and treating them with irresistible importance.

When I refer to a "best friend," I don't mean it in the childish, momentary sense. Many of these delightful individuals remained my friends for decades—and some still are. So, although I enjoyed my own company, even as a child, I understood that I inherently needed more.

That's not to suggest being constantly solitary was all sunshine, rainbows, and unicorns. Being alone as a child much of the time failed to teach me how to embrace, adeptly move through, and transmute painful experiences. In that realm of personal healing, being on my own was an enormous handicap. Like most of us, I had a tendency to get stuck in those hurtful or confusing situations, both mentally and emotionally.

My creativity and my inner reflection could become morose at times. This was especially true as I hit my teen years. I had no idea how to share my inner struggles with my friends. I felt utterly and terminally unique, believing no one could possibly understand my pain fully.

As one of my personal spiritual guides, Rev. Dr. David Ault, often says, "Your pain is not special." He didn't invent that idea, but I heard it from him first, and it challenged me, as I know it can challenge many of us. The specialness of my own experience of pain remains a seductive idea to me.

Of course, the truth is, *I am special*. What is not special is my pain. The illusion that we are alone, misunderstood, and disconnected is very common and pervasive—especially during times when we are hurting.

I have watched another spiritual guide of mine, Kathryn, gently slide a note to someone who is suffering emotionally, even if she barely knows them. On the note it simply says: "You are not alone." The impact of that tiny note is universally enormous.

Once I was sitting together with her and a dear friend who was going through a messy divorce. During the conversation, true to form, Kathryn slid the familiar note across the table. My friend looked down and read it, then instantly burst into tears. That was precisely how she had been feeling—utterly, horribly alone, even though loving support surrounded her. Our circumstances often cannot penetrate our inner story and trauma, unless someone like David or Kathryn intervenes and challenges our perception.

This why we rarely can make a major shift effectively on our own. Quite plainly, we are generally unable to manage our thoughts all alone, all the time. They are our thoughts, and we have no real perspective on them.

We need one another to help us see ourselves more clearly—especially during times of major shift. If you have been reading attentively, you might feel like this statement is in conflict with some of the statements made in chapter 1. Didn't I declare earlier that we couldn't be defined by other people's opinions, and that we should trust ourselves, first and foremost? Now here I am saying I can't be trusted to help myself, and I require other people to help me see clearly! Which is it, crazy lady?

The answer is, frustratingly, "It depends." It depends on how difficult you are finding it to make a particular shift. Remember the example of taking a trip. Because travel is a small shift for most people, we go through that shift with relative ease. We might ask someone who has already been to our intended destination about their experience and insights. Their view is appreciated, but we make the decision ourselves, with relative ease. In that instance, if someone inserted themselves into our decision process without our asking for advice, it would be unwelcome interference.

However, let's suppose you have never traveled abroad, and, though you want to, you find yourself to unable to take the first action to move forward. You are stuck in the hallway. That is the time when you want another perspective. Whether it is travel or anything else, your dream is within your reach when you allow yourself to be guided—and, most importantly, guided by someone who has had a successful experience with precisely that thing. It is nonnegotiable that whoever it is, it must be a person whom you can trust.

THE TRUSTED GUIDE

There are a number of ways to tell if someone can be trusted. Unfortunately, many of us have trusted the wrong individuals. We chose people who, for whatever reason, could not be a reliable guide for us. It can be very damaging.

Just because someone is your parent, spouse, co-worker, or teacher does not mean they can guide you through a particular shift you are undertaking. Major shifts require the disassembling of deeply held beliefs that parents and spouses, for example, may have unwittingly helped you to build in the first place! Even if they didn't help build your limiting beliefs, the vulnerability major shifting requires can feel overwhelming to unpack in front of these people whose opinions matter so much. In brief—working with them can be debilitating.

The guides who actually can be trusted for a major shift have these attributes in common:

1. They are neutral. Your relationship with them is not highly charged and does not depend on your ability to successfully shift.
2. They demonstrate their belief in you to do this for yourself.
3. They have been in a similar, if not identical, situation at some point and are at least a little bit ahead of you in the process. They get where you are because they have been there too.
4. They are not going to judge you, criticize you, or give you tons of advice. They allow you to find your own way, mostly by sharing what worked for them or others. They offer up their experiences, suggesting things you can try.
5. They will call you out on your rationalizations, denial, and excuses, even if it makes you angry. They will love you in spite of your reaction, without taking it personally.
6. They provide inspiration and hope, as well as a shoulder to cry on when it gets really rough.
7. They treat you with the respect you sometimes forget to give yourself.

8. They listen extremely well—sometimes better than you listen to yourself—and reflect back to you what they are hearing.

9. There are no secrets between you. Any topic that needs to be discussed can be, so they may see you in your fullness as the amazing individual you are, warts and all.

10. They don't promise magical solutions (an unfortunately common misrepresentation of guidance these days) such as shedding twenty-five pounds in one week or tripling your income in a month.

If this description sounds impossibly narrow, be aware, this is precisely what certified coaches, therapists, ministers, twelve-step sponsors, and business consultants are expected to both know and do. The reason is simple: they are the first line of defense when someone is going through a major shift. Your own guide doesn't need to be a trained expert, although they can be. It is crucial to know what to look for, and that it does exist.

Trained professionals are also human (shocking, I know!) and will occasionally slip up, performing their role imperfectly, giving unsolicited advice, delivering what sounds like a harsh criticism, or just not being all that supportive. Their humanity is not your engraved invitation to bail on your shift in disgust, returning to the shelter of your hallway.

However, if your chosen guide slips up regularly, they are demonstrating they are not trustworthy to you. Your job then is to make a different choice and find a better guide, or admit you just aren't ready for what this shift demands of you. Remember, you chose your guide. You gravitate towards the guide that will respond perfectly to your level of willingness to change. And you can rechoose any time you need to do so.

I personally have several guides simultaneously. I think of them as my committee. Each one has prominence in a particular area of my life. I have one whom I lean on for guidance in my relationships, because I was a tough case! That's Kathryn. She is happily married, for many decades, and has been through many of the same relationship hurdles I have faced. She knows everything about me, and she calls me on my messy thinking when it surfaces.

Another guides me in my career. Still another guides me in the realm of intuition. I don't lean on all of them at once, but I know they are there when I need to dig a little deeper. Only one of my guides is a professional.

THE MASTERS

Besides a personal guide there are also those I call "the masters." They are in the realm of the self-help gurus. Self-help, like this book, has real value. It demonstrates that successful transformation is possible, and so it gives us hope and a roadmap. It is inspiring, challenging, and often extremely practical. Where it gets a bad rap is twofold:

First, many of us expect the self-help guru to do it for us. Many books, videos, courses, workshops, and seminars are built on this idea, unfortunately. The information each one contains is typically accurate and also incomplete. I have yet to meet the individual who studied an amazing author, or even attended an extensive in-person course, and made a dramatic shift overnight by osmosis.

Nonetheless, we still seek an easy transformation we just pop into our brains, and presto!—we are remade in the image of the self-help guru, like magic. When that doesn't happen, we get irritated and say their program doesn't work—or at least it doesn't work for us.

Stage 8 of *Shift* is "Plan to Practice." We must practice what we have learned on a regular basis in order for shift to occur. Only we can do that.

When we are faced with a major resistance in a shift, going it alone (a.k.a. "helping ourselves") has most likely not worked. There is little or no feedback other that self-assessment in self-help. It is excruciatingly difficult, if not impossible, to heal our own limiting beliefs in isolation. Our stories and our perspectives are distorted enough that we need someone other than ourselves to walk through a shift with us.

Most self-help gurus make a nice living being that guide to anyone who can pay their fees. There is nothing wrong with that. However, if that is outside your means, take the classes, read the books, get inspired by the demonstration of transformation. Just don't stop there.

Use the information provided by the master and find a guide, in the form of an individual or a supportive group, to help you get there by ensuring you can also see through your blind spots.

The second component of self-help's bad rap is the mercenaries. This is, unfortunately, becoming quite common. As a result, we must choose our master as carefully as we choose our trusted guides. In fact, some masters are out there doing more harm than they are doing good. They even can overshadow the true masters. The more discerning we are of what we choose to believe, the more usefulness we will be able to gain from the self-help that is available.

Self-help is the best way I know to increase your knowledge and awareness when you are ready to undertake a major shift. I encourage you to dive in. Explore everything you can find. Next you're going to need to develop the wisdom and skill to make your dream into a reality. For me, this always begins with learning.

THE TRIBE

Even better than self-help, and especially when used in combination with it, is the experience of others. Learn from those individuals who have been where you are or are headed where you want to be. The wisdom found in a group that is working on the same shift is so important.

No two people experience the world is exactly the same way. By being in community with individuals who share their unique perspectives, we begin the journey of practicing a new way of being. We lean on one another, learn from one another, and even see first-hand what not to do.

There's one important component that differentiates a tribe from other social gatherings: commitment. A tribe is committed to its fellow members and requires some level of accountability for showing up regularly to support one another. This is what creates a safe space for vulnerability. If a gathering doesn't require that level of commitment, there is very little continuity or depth of intimacy among members. Without commitment, accountability, safety, and intimacy, what we learn is unreliable.

Effective tribes can be found in support groups, Facebook groups, forums, churches, classrooms, and associations. They also can be lacking in those same places. What you are looking for is shared focus that matches yours, support, experience, accountability, commitment, safety, and willingness to be vulnerable with each other. When one of those is missing, your tribe is likely to be less helpful to you.

A trusted guide, master, and tribe are complementary to each other, and all three are essential for successful shift. A tribe without a master or trusted guide easily devolves into the blind leading the blind. A master without a tribe or trusted advisor is a theory with no practice to support it. And a trusted guide, without a master or a tribe, lacks direction.

We must immerse ourselves in our shift. We must find our hope and inspiration and then dive into the midst of countless others on the same transformational journey. It is like learning a new language. You might get the theory behind it on your own, but until you live in the midst of a culture where it is continuously spoken by everyone, it is too easy to revert to your native tongue, simply because it is familiar.

Being amid others who speak the language you want to speak is a sure way to see vividly how you are doing. Their responses to you provide vital feedback. Be open to it. As our shift takes hold we can quickly become overconfident in early stages. You can minimize the risk of premature action if you remain humble. A master, a guide, and a tribe provide the feedback we absolutely must have to proceed. Feedback is essential for progress.

EXERCISES TO CONNECT

Exercise 1: Google, the Great Tribe Builder

Whether you are embarrassed about the shift you want to make (for example, you are struggling with debt or addiction) or are just clueless about what is available, let the great Google search engine point the way. There are more than fifty-two twelve-step recovery programs currently. Some are bigger and have greater reach than others, but there is likely to be one for exactly what you struggle with, if it relates to addiction. There are even several for people addicted to relationships with people who have an addiction!

There are countless Meet-Ups, workshops, churches of any denomination, or simply spiritual communities without a denomination, and there are retreats happening every day of the year. If there isn't one in your area that seems to fit, then you can find a version of it online, guaranteed.

The coaching industry is also exploding. Although it is currently unregulated, if you look carefully, there are excellent certifying entities such as the International Coaches Federation that ensure a high level of professionalism and ethical standards. There are life, spiritual, business, finance, growth, health, relationship, parenting, life transition, retirement, career, and countless other sorts of coaches. There is certain to be one for you if you choose to go that route.

So start searching and exploring what is available to you in these areas and any other area. Attend something, call someone, explore, and, if it doesn't fit, try something else. One thing is certain—when you begin to look, your focus is on positive transformation, and your own energy will already begin to shift.

Exercise 2: Get Out of Your Own Routine

If we are struggling to find a guide, tribe or master, then it is likely we have been keeping a particular focus that prevents us discovering what we need. One focus is isolating ourselves, which doesn't connect us with others at all. Another reason we might struggle is that we keep our selves too busy with our work and a narrow group of friends and thus we are prevented from new interactions and experiences. A third is that we have a certain tribe we already are extremely comfortable with, but it doesn't provide the support we need in a particular area.

So plan and schedule to broaden your reach, whether it is directly related to your desired shift or not. Take a trip, visit a different association than you typically would, or hang out with those neighbors you rarely speak to who seem so nice. As you broaden your connections and your routine, you will find you are naturally drawn to the exact groups and individuals you have been needing. Remember, this is not a race. It is a process of discovery.

Exercise 3: Ask for Help

Some of us are really horrible when it comes to asking for help. If you are like me, you were taught how important self-sufficiency is. Asking for help to those like us is to risk losing our autonomy, being seen as needy, or worse, being let down. Others believe asking for help shows fatal weakness. Both of those extreme views are rarely born out. But there is a caveat—depending on the help you need, there will be people who are not safe to ask for help.

Even so, asking for help can absolutely be safely done in the confidence of a professional counselor or coach. It likely can be done with a friend or mentor—although an individual who doesn't know us as well can often be easier to ask. Regardless, the hardest action we ever take when we are ready to own our own shift is to admit to another human being exactly what we are trying to do, and that we need help to do it.

So, if you must, practice first. Every day, practice asking whatever invisible Presence you can subscribe to (God, Spirit, Nature, the Universe), "Presence, I am seeking help in making this shift. Can you guide me?" Then thank the Presence, and go about your day or fall asleep soundly.

You might be surprised what happens next in two ways: First, when you ask enough, the asking becomes easier and more natural in every relationship you are in. Second, for whatever reason, when we begin to ask, we also begin to receive help.

There are many theories about this phenomenon. My belief is our own energy and awareness shifts, and we become more open and receptive. Our focus subliminally moves to the search for guidance, and, lo and behold, the guidance we have been looking for appears! (It was always there, but we weren't looking for it.) Others say the Presence of God responds. And to that I ask, what if the two answers might actually be one and the same?

CHAPTER THREE

SURRENDER

WHATEVER YOU WANT can be yours—when you are willing to give up whatever stands in your way. That is the underlying principle of surrender. We aren't giving in to something outside ourselves. We are opening up to something inside ourselves. Surrender is like throwing open the door to infinity, where all things are possible. It is incredible. It is also incredibly disorienting. To pass through the door, we only need to let go of everything familiar that we thought we knew.

When we surrender, we stop resisting reality, since whatever we resist, persists. By resisting "what is" we paradoxically hold it firmly in place. Then, suddenly, we let go, taking our foot off the brake, and we are free. Surrender creates enormous freedom. So why is it often so disorienting and so difficult?

THE LAW OF SACRIFICE

In metaphysics there are a number of laws that operate on our experiences, just as physical scientific laws do. One of these is the Law of Sacrifice. It states:

In order to receive something greater, you must give up something lesser.

We are always using this law—either intentionally or unintentionally. If you run a business, you may have to reallocate your resources in order to generate greater visibility or profit. In your relationships, you may need to give up judging and criticizing in order to gain greater respect and intimacy. Both of these are examples of giving up something lesser to allow something greater to be created.

Whatever it is that you will need to shift, deep beneath the surface there is a belief you are attached to that is holding you back. This is where get stuck. We won't let go of these limiting beliefs—about our unworthiness, scarcity, conflict, abuses, and so many other ideas we formed long ago. Since we typically formed these beliefs early in our lives, we have little conscious awareness of when or why we made them. They may have even protected us (or we felt like they did) from emotional or physical harm. But now they are not helping us at all.

It is time to let them go.

This is the key to surrendering. We recognize that what we have been holding onto is no longer working for us. It is actually doing more harm than good. We have tried countless things to change, yet no matter what we try, the pattern continues. Now we are at the point where, exhausted, we finally just let go. We surrender.

We aren't letting go of our life. We are letting go of the fight. We stop holding our breath and relax. Deep down we realize that all our willpower and our attempts to outwit the situation were never the answer. For this moment, we are ready to allow a power greater than us—whether that is a divine presence, our guide, our master, or our tribe—to take the wheel.

This is the stage where we finally change our minds and trust that something greater is possible. Surrender is an incredibly hopeful act.

ASKING FOR HELP

I cannot recommend strongly enough that you find a support network before you surrender. That is why this chapter comes after the previous one. There are examples of individuals who have successfully had breakthroughs after surrendering on their own. The Buddha is one such example. It took him forty-nine days of straight meditation and many years of trying ascetic living before he fully surrendered.

You can certainly try to let go alone, like the Buddha, but for most of us mere mortals, that rarely leads to surrender. Instead it leads to free-fall. And free-fall is traumatic. It is especially traumatic if you have never done it before. I know this firsthand.

I jumped out of my first, last, and only airplane at age twenty-four. At the end of an insanely stressful week, on the way to the Georgia skydiving drop zone that my first husband, Mark, an experienced skydiver, frequented, I decided, "What the hell? I need to really get out of my comfort zone! I'll jump too!"

That decision might sound absolutely random and insane to

many readers, but each of us has our tipping point and our response to it. I had reached mine. I was ready to let go of my stress, and the best way I knew of in that moment was to let go of my fears at work by facing the fear of jumping. That emotional state I was in is a common, fertile ground for surrender.

There I was. The plane door was open. The wind and the plane engines were so loud you could barely hear if someone yelled at the top of their lungs, so hand signals were necessary. We were cruising at fifteen thousand feet, so the air was thin, and we didn't have a lot of time to hang out at that level. One after the other we inched towards the door, and one after the other we tumbled out. My husband was on the flight with me somewhere behind us. He had jumped hundreds of times.

But at the moment, I was harnessed to another man—my tandem master, who had spent thirty minutes with me before we got on the plane, teaching me how to "arch" by lying on my belly on the hanger floor—which resembled an advanced yoga move—and how to keep my center of gravity pointing at the earth at all times.

"That's all you need to know," he told me. "If you can do that, then everything else will be fine. I'll watch the altimeter, pull the chute's ripcord—and, here, please sign these waiver forms that describe a number of possible ways you will not experience death by falling."

I was given a jumpsuit and fitted into a harness that was designed to connect to my instructor's.

And now here we were at the door of the plane. The person in front of us gave the person at the door the thumbs up, and then just fell out of the plane. That made us next. I was in front, with a full view of the bluish-greenish earth below. My goggles were on, the roar was in my ears, and I am pretty sure I had stopped breathing.

Then the thumbs up signal happened again, between the guy at the door and my tandem master, and one of them pushed me out the door.

Now, freeze.

Time stops when you're in free-fall.

I flew in slow motion out of the door, and the overload on my senses was nearly indescribable. I was aware. Aware that I was hurtling towards the earth at terminal velocity of 120 miles per hour.

But that's not how it felt.

It felt like floating.

The air came at me so fast that now I couldn't breathe if I chose to. It had the consistency of water. There was no frame of reference that I was falling. Other skydivers, like my husband, managed to navigate around us and they were falling at the same rate, so the illusion was that none of us were falling at all.

Since I had not left the house with the intention to skydive that day, I had on my slip-on Keds, which were flapping wildly on my feet like they were about to fly away in the wind. All I could think about was them landing on some poor farmer's head. And it was about that point my tandem master yelled in my ear that I needed to remember to arch.

The cameraman came into view and started floating around us, giving me a high five, which made my arch even worse. Arching correctly was my only job. And I was blowing it. We were tumbling now. Was I going to kill us both?

Then, BAM!

Our chute opened and we suddenly flew up—or it appeared that way—since our fall had stopped.

That's when I saw the world fully for the first time, softly un-focused and intensely green in the sun. The roar of planes and wind was gone and there was just silence except for the rippling of the chute in the air. I was flying with nothing between myself and infinity. It was beyond words—and so we said nothing during the twenty-minute canopy ride.

As we came into the landing, the chute leveled out and we slid forward into some grass. What followed this was disbelief and shock. Then euphoria.

I had flown. It was flying like I only know from my dreams. That euphoria and awe is the natural result of surrender—when you have a guide. Imagine the horrible—even fatal—result, had I tried to jump on my own. What would have happened if I had not understood my instructions? What if the sensory overload was too much for me and I passed out, as many people do? What if I was not able to arch successfully and spun out of control? The list goes on and on.

I suspect many people confuse free-fall with surrender. As a result, surrender gets a bad rap. There is certainly a free-fall component to it, but it is not the entire experience. There is the weightless quality, the glimpse into infinity, as well as a return to solid ground.

A guide, master, and tribe hold us, and reassure us, in the intensely vulnerable place surrender creates. They encourage us, steer us on how to keep our center of gravity during the process, and sometimes even push us out of the plane when we hesitate. For these reasons, and many more, I encourage you to ask for help during the stage of surrender. It will not protect you from the free-fall experience, but it will ensure you are able to safely land.

THE TIME TO SURRENDER

We are constantly making small surrenders we aren't even aware of.

We surrender our routine in order to travel. We surrender certain ways of eating when we are ready to lose weight or address certain medical conditions. We throw open the door to infinite possibility and temporary disorientation. We do it in order to experience one aspect of personal freedom that we have until that point not had.

Since the more important an activity is to your soul's evolution, the more resistance there is to it, it's also true that the bigger the opportunity for freedom, the more we try to avoid what is required to claim it.

There are various signs that it is time for us to surrender, willingly or not:

1. Overwhelm
2. Exhaustion
3. Illness
4. Resentment
5. Restlessness
6. Frustration
7. Anxiety
8. Indecision/doubt
9. Disappointment
10. Chronic patterns

If we experience any of the preceding signs in a heightened, extended manner, we are on a collision course with surrender, either by choice (recommended) or by force (rather painful). The force comes in the form of unbearable consequences from our current actions and mindsets.

WHAT DOES SURRENDER LOOK LIKE?

Surrender is one of the most natural, simple things in the world. We relax, and we exhale. We roll out the door of the plane. We admit that our battle against our current reality has been part of the problem.

In practical terms, we see things as they really are. If the job is unreasonably demanding, we become aware and accept that. If we have a particular addiction, we acknowledge it is controlling our life and admit our dependency. If our relationship involves infidelity or abuse, we stop denying the obvious signs.

That is all that there is to surrender. See it. Accept it. No denial. No immediate action. Just realize the reality of the situation. When we do that, we also recognize that nothing we have tried up to this point to alter the situation has worked. We are in a state of relaxed acceptance.

Surely there is more? That's too easy! I must have left something out.

I did not.

When you realize that recognition is all there is to surrender, then why not go there alone? The reason is we are usually ill equipped to handle what comes next. Your whole ego construct is built on resistance, and the rug just got pulled out from under it. Right now your ego is now about to start the fight of your life. You are going to need reinforcements.

EXERCISE TO PREPARE FOR SURRENDER

When we are stuck and ready to shift, there is always a tell-tale sign. For each of the following, make a note of whether it applies to you. If it does, write down what you are resisting that creates the discomfort. For example, if you are feeling overwhelmed, it arises from resisting something. You might be resisting missing a deadline or letting someone down. What is it that you are resisting enough to cause feeling overwhelmed? What would happen to you if you stopped resisting? (Write in your answers after the colons.)

1. I am feeling overwhelmed:_____
    I am resisting:_____
    If I stopped resisting, then:_____

2. I am feeling exhaustion:_____
    I am resisting:_____
    If I stopped resisting, then:_____

3. I am feeling illness:_____
    I am resisting:_____
    If I stopped resisting, then:_____

4. I am feeling resentment:_____
    I am resisting:_____
    If I stopped resisting, then:_____

5. I am feeling restlessness:_____
    I am resisting:_____
    If I stopped resisting, then:_____

6. I am feeling frustration:_____

   I am resisting:_____

   If I stopped resisting, then:_____

7. I am feeling anxiety:_____

   I am resisting:_____

   If I stopped resisting, then:_____

8. I am feeling indecision/doubt:_____

   I am resisting:_____

   If I stopped resisting, then:_____

9. I am feeling disappointment:_____

   I am resisting:_____

   If I stopped resisting, then:_____

10. I am experiencing chronic patterns:_____

   I am resisting:_____

   If I stopped resisting, then:_____

CHAPTER FOUR

TRUST THE FIRE WITHIN

WE KNOW MORE THAN WE THINK WE DO. Learn to trust the fire within.

Suppose you are driving down the road in your car on a wild, stormy night, when you pass by a bus stop and you see three people waiting for the bus: an old lady who looks as if she is about to die, an old friend who once saved your life, and the perfect partner you have been dreaming about.

Knowing that there can only be one passenger in your car, whom would you choose to help?

Riddles like this one challenge our assumptions about the world we live in. The way this riddle is phrased assumes you are the kind-hearted type who would actually want to help all three individuals.

It's rarely the case in real life that there is only one right answer, but we act as if that is the case. As the riddle solvers, we also have been taught to assume there is one right answer. Of course, there is the answer the designer of the riddle wants us to reach. However, I will show you in a moment when even the "right" answer is based on a number of assumptions. They plague us constantly.

The best way to solve any riddle is to begin asking more questions, because, by their very nature, riddles obscure the answer(s). Simple and powerful questions like: What do we know about this situation? What don't we know?

The predetermined answer to this riddle is quite elegant: You get out of the car, hand the keys to your friend, help the old lady into the passenger seat, and wait at the bus stop with your perfect partner.

Let's look at the assumptions in this answer! It assumes you are physically in good health. It assumes the friend can drive. It assumes the bus will arrive (hopefully sooner rather than later.) Nonetheless, it is a good, delightfully creative answer if all those things are indeed true.

Solving riddles is a remarkable skill. It does not depend on having greater intelligence. What it does demand is perspective and insight, which is not directly correlated with intelligence. Our brains contain many levels of thinking. The one we culturally assign higher credibility to is rational, logical thought. This type of thinking represents on about 10 percent of our cognitive and decision-making process.

What we are talking about is the difference between linear (or vertical) thinking and lateral thinking, which were described by Edward de Bono in 1970. Our society embraces and rewards vertical (rational, logical) thinking very highly.

Logical thinking approaches problems by being selective,

analytical, and sequential. Any process built on the scientific method relies on logical thinking.

Our deep cultural bias towards logical thinking shows up in our educational system and thus has trained our executive leadership in one particular style of problem solving. We see logic and scientific method as infallible. More subtly, we have come to believe that there is only a single right solution, one validated by external facts and data—and one that, most notably, is primarily focused on avoiding failure.

On the other hand, lateral thinking takes a completely different approach. Lateral thinking resides in our unconscious and subconscious mind. It represents roughly 90 percent of our mental processes. It does not exclude logic, but it adds intuition, creativity, and imagination through unconscious and subconscious processes. In short, lateral thinking allows for more than one solution. Lateral thinking also decides from internal guidance, without requiring external data.

Lateral thinking, when taught to young children, has benefits that improve overall well-being for the rest of their lives. These include, but are not limited to:

- Achieving stability both socially and emotionally
- Developing physiological maturity at a younger age
- Limiting levels of anger and aggression
- Performing at a higher level in classrooms
- Improving personal and professional life

With a list like that, it would seem like a good idea to encourage and reward greater lateral problem solving over logical problem solving. But the preceding riddle is an example of a lateral thinking riddle that, unless you have heard it before (no cheating) you are likely to find yourself at least stumbling on.

Lateral thinking requires intuition.

People who are able to make intuitive leaps can quickly recognize solutions that their peers may miss. Riddles are the perfect puzzle to train not only young children, but also adults seeking to build intuitive ability and make better, faster decisions. As with anything, new thoughts and behaviors require practice, and riddles provide exactly that—practice for thinking differently.

THE STILL, SMALL VOICE

The most common question I hear from my students is: How can I trust my intuition?

Although these students are curious, they have little confidence that they ever can trust their intuitive understanding. Intuition has been proven to exist, and it often provides faster, more accurate decisions, but our society has not caught up to that science yet.

Most people don't typically recognize their intuition unless the still, small voice becomes much louder and insistent or, worse, something goes very wrong. Instead they belatedly realize intuition had been sounding an alarm in a language they just could not comprehend. Frequently, intuitive insight feels unpredictable, unreliable, and frustratingly unhelpful. In fact, intuition seems to have a mind of its own!

Nothing could be further from the truth. Intuition serves us faithfully. It is constantly providing guidance and offering up solutions to our much slower, logical mind. In order to get out of the hallway of a particularly sticky shift, we must learn to recognize its presence, hear its messages, and follow where it leads us, because it is us. There is no separation between the conscious us and the subconscious us. It is all one mind—our own. Our job is to leverage the connection between the two aspects of our mind so they function synchronously.

Intuition is a person's capacity to obtain or have direct knowledge and/or immediate insight, without observation or reason. It's the "gut feeling" you get. People who do trust their intuition place an enormous amount of faith on it, even making decisions that seem to go against all available evidence. The key to recognizing when it is intuition instead of our fears or desires guiding us is the level of emotion. Intuition has no emotion attached to it. It simply knows.

Intuition is a powerful aid in our discernment and decision making. There is research that demonstrates the power and accuracy of this process, and that we always use it prior to any analytic process—without consciousness of the process. When you are also aware of your own internal, unfinished business that can block intuition, when you recognize that we tend to be influenced by what's familiar, shying away from what's uncomfortable, then you will be better able to create a channel for your intuition past the noise of habitual thoughts and biases.

INTUITION-BUILDING PRACTICES

There are many practices that help you to access your intuition and strengthen the ability to access it on demand, with reliable results. Whichever ones you try, know that your intuition will respond to the degree that you commit to connecting to it. The more you practice, the more you will meet your intuition and recognize its presence, because you opened up to it. Here are the most common practices:

Creativity: Ironically we tend to put limitations on what we categorize as creativity. It is much more than artistic talents. Just like the riddles at the beginning of the chapter, solving problems is one creative activity. Others include cooking, gardening, teaching, parenting, building, or engineering.

Mindfulness: This is simply the art of being fully present and aware. In 1979, Jon Kabat-Zinn is credited with bringing the practice to the United States, but it originated in Eastern Hindu practices. It is not only a practice to strengthen intuition, it is also an incredible stress reduction technique, and often used to help heal chronic illnesses and ease pain.

You can practice mindfulness at any time, with any activity. Although it is typically associated with meditation, you can practice it while eating, walking, playing an instrument, or driving your car. All it requires is to be consciously focused on and aware of your body, its sensations, your breath, and how your mind tends to wander. For short periods of time you notice all this and gently redirect your thoughts back to your body and the present activity. For more ideas and mindfulness techniques, go to mindful.org.

Observe everything: This is often referred to as "high noticing" and is a multisensory practice. Like mindfulness, this is a practice that can be eased into, beginning with just a few minutes initially.

Hear the birds in the background or a conversation at the table next to you. Feel the light breeze or the texture of your clothing. See the clouds passing overhead or the feather on the ground at your feet.

The difference between this practice and mindfulness is that in mindfulness you are aware of you and your thoughts, while, in this activity, you are noticing your outer experience.

Listen to your body: When we have pain or tension it is natural to want to relieve the symptoms quickly. When we are on a deadline and not getting enough sleep, we often grab a cup of coffee or other stimulant in order to keep going. Sometimes these responses to our bodies are unavoidable.

This is not a practice of avoiding responsibility or being in unbearable discomfort. It is a practice of being aware that our bodies are telling us what they need and, as soon as possible, providing comfort and care to ourselves.

Our bodies are a powerful channel for our intuition, but only if we are already in a practice of paying attention to them.

Practice compassion for others: Empathy as a practice expands our consciousness and awareness. It shifts our thoughts (usually linear) to feelings (usually lateral). It also reduces the ego's self-absorption, and self-consumed focus.

Compassion for others is about recognizing how they might feel, not attempting to fix or manage their feelings. It is important to keep your compassion lovingly detached, allowing the other person to have their own feelings for themselves. This maintains your own emotional health and well-being as well as the other's.

Pay attention to dreams: Dreams are some of the most useful sources of insight when you begin connecting to your intuition. There are many schools of thought about the meaning (or lack of meaning) in dreams. My personal stance is that the imagery and situations contained within the dream are outside the rigorous control of our logical mind, and so they contain a tremendous amount of metaphorical, symbolic insight. I have found that when I write my dreams down, the metaphors—and even puns—make themselves obvious very quickly.

Occasionally I will look up a particular symbolic meaning of an animal, object, or place. It is not that dreams have created the meaning, but rather that, culturally, we share a common mythology. As a westerner, I am more likely to resonate with western symbology, for example.

What's more, as I am writing dreams down, or researching symbolic meanings, I am also checking in with myself. I inquire: Does this sound right? Or is there something off? What does this bring up for me? Does it remind me of something? Are memories or thoughts that seem unrelated being triggered? In short, I am asking my intuition to help me understand what it is telling me.

Find time to relax and be still: Essentially this is a mindfulness practice—just hitting the pause button for a moment.

We live in an overstimulated and distracted world. All the more reason to make stillness and being fully present a priority. Many people like that idea in theory but struggle to understand how to create it for themselves. When we are still for the first time in a long time, instead of relief, we feel anxiety—as if something is wrong. This is merely unfamiliarity, and a bit of stimulation-withdrawal.

By pushing through the initial discomfort, we begin to connect with a deeper sense of ourselves, and a sense there is a much deeper self-contained within us. We are right. That is the 90 percent of us that is below our consciousness. In stillness, we can connect. All it takes initially is just a few minutes a day.

Let go of negative emotions: This can be the most difficult practice of all for most of us. Our brains are biased towards negativity, and the bulk of our daily thoughts are negative. Not only that, they are repetitive. Letting go of them is another mindfulness practice, which simply involves paying more attention and then shifting your focus.

For example, suppose you are thinking about a co-worker who has been critical and combative, and you are experiencing stress over it. First, notice you are thinking about the situation, and notice your feelings about it are negative: "Oh. I'm thinking about Bob again, and it's stressing me out. It's like I'm having the experience all over again." Then point your mind elsewhere. You could do a gratitude list or go for a short walk. The first brings in positive ideas without stuffing any you might have about Bob, while the second provides stress release of movement and a change of scene—again, without stuffing or denying any feelings about Bob.

Letting go of negative emotions is never an act of denial or avoidance, but of refocusing and replacing. There is certainly more extensive work possible here for older and deeper negative beliefs, but for now, this helps open you up for intuitive guidance—especially the creative inspirations that could help you deal with your co-worker Bob, who sounds like he could use some of this himself.

INTUITION INHIBITORS

The greatest stumbling block to intuition is our own thinking. We have such a bias towards figuring out solutions logically that we regularly overlook the possibility of inspiration, and, when it arises anyway, we mistrust it. Instead we focus on researching our options, discussing the situation with others, and attempting to consider an endless array of future outcomes. In other words, we overthink things a lot, which creates so much mental noise we can't hear intuition if it is screaming in our ear. At its worst, this creates analysis paralysis.

The next obstacle to intuition is our belief-based allegiance to how things should be or how they ought to happen. These "shoulds" can also apply to us, to what we are even allowing ourselves to do or consider.

Remember the riddles. There are more situations that refuse to obey our self-imposed shoulds than not. Creative solutions are typically elegant and break normal parameters. After all, if normal parameters worked, there wouldn't be an issue.

Another inhibitor is our desire to adhere to an authority figure's needs, wants, opinion, or advice. We trust their opinions and stance over our own—or, at least, we don't trust ourselves.

The authority factor can also block us if we are reacting against it as well. Whether we are rebelling or trying to please, the authority's influence is determining our approach more than our own internal guidance system. The result is, once again, the small, still voice of intuition gets drowned out.

Also, any time we have a strong desire or attachment to a particular outcome, we shut down all other possibilities—including those that might arise out of our intuition. The latter, arising from our massive subconscious well of resources, has an annoying tendency to present options that are even better and more powerful than our original, consciously devised plan. Like the voice at the Sedona vortex saying, "It is time for you to go out on your own," I was presented with an option so radical, I would not have even considered it without intuitive inspiration.

Lastly, and sadly, past traumas, especially those from our childhoods, shut down many feelings and the intuitive insight that comes through feeling. The protective numbing we create for ourselves from pain we were too vulnerable to feel as children must be healed in order to have full access to intuition's power. If this is something that resonates with you, I encourage you to seek healing therapy before going further in this book. While I certainly understand and empathize, this is best dealt with in a professional, therapeutic relationship.

INTUITION TOOLS

There are countless ways to build our intuitive muscle. Each of us is unique in what we find most effective. I personally use a variety, interchangeably and as they present themselves—including dreams, recognizing and interpreting signs and symbols, sensing my clairsentience ("clear feeling") and following where it leads me, ritual, and meditation.

If you are new to intentionally activating your intuitive connection, that might sound like an awful lot of work. However, I am not suggesting that you try all of this at once, nor that you need to spend an enormous amount of time on it before continuing. I encourage you to explore on your own and plan to practice regularly.

EXERCISES TO STRENGTHEN INTUITION

Exercise 1: Lucid Dreaming

Lucid dreaming is a dream state where we are dreaming while we are aware that it is a dream. The conscious and subconscious mind are in heightened connectivity as a result. When this state is achieved, the dreamer can exert control over what occurs in the dream. For those who have no awareness of their dreams at all, I suggest you begin with the exercise anyway, and stick with it. Dreams will begin to arise in your memory in bits and pieces and grow more pronounced as you continue the exercise.

Keep a dream journal: One of the best, easiest, fastest ways to create a pattern of lucid dreaming is to keep a dream journal. Even if you currently have little or no recollection of your dream life, the dream journal will establish the awareness of what is happening while you are literally sleeping.

It is generally recommended to keep a separate journal beside your bed and train yourself to immediately write down what you can remember upon waking. I have found it more productive to lie in the dark with my eyes closed upon waking and do a mental scan for the subtle threads of dreams, and then solidify them before the disruption of getting up and turning on the light.

The key is to make your dream journal a habit. The more regularly you establish the connection between conscious and subconscious activities, the more readily it occurs. I personally kept a dream journal for one semester, and by the end of the semester I was remembering so many dreams (more than thirty each night) that I had to stop writing or I would have spent all day at it.

Be absolutely nonjudgmental about your dreams. They simply are. Observe, write them down, and, if they stir up curiosity or interest, go ahead and explore the symbolism that is present. Your interpretations are exactly that—interpretations. See where they lead you.

Lastly, an extremely powerful catalyst for lucid dreaming is to set your intention before you fall asleep: I will dream and be aware I am dreaming tonight. This works best if you do it just as you are losing full consciousness and repeat it each night.

It also bears noting that our culture is notoriously sleep deprived, and lucid dreaming is most accessible when you are getting the proper amount of rest regularly.

Exercise 2: Activate the Download

We all have moments when we get an inner sense of knowing. It is often referred to as "the still, small voice." The hallmark of the voice is that it is not associated with any emotion. It is simply pure awareness. I refer to this as "the download" and believe it represents my intuition surfacing with a clear direction.

Here are some of the most common ways it will show up for us universally:

- **People:** A person keeps crossing our mind, and we feel we should connect with them without a specific reason.

- **Places:** We have lost something or are on our way to somewhere and we feel compelled to look in a particular place or go a certain route.

- **Things:** We have a vague sense that something is not right in combination with the idea to check something out, such as an appliance, account, vehicle, device, document, etc. We have not received any conscious signals of a problem, but we can't shake the feeling.

- **Situations:** It doesn't/does feel right. With little or no information to go on, we have a strong feeling about our next hire, a potential home, our health or well-being, a trip we are planning, and so on.

- **Creativity/experimenting:** Sometimes the inner direction may suggest we try something out of the ordinary, such as a different route to our destination, or a new hobby. It might be as mundane as the idea of what line to get in at the grocery store. (Most of us resist this.)

- **Problem Solving:** Counter-rational solutions may pop into our minds when we give our rational mind a break, such as while driving a familiar route, showering, taking a walk, or doing something that we don't need to concentrate on.

All of these are what is referred to as "the download," and you a can build the download frequency, reliability, and reliance by practicing. It is quite easy. On a daily basis, give yourself a choice that has low risk. Perhaps choosing that grocery store line after all, or which route you will take to your destination. Ask yourself: Which one?

Only don't try to answer intellectually. Drop down into the realm of feeling—which is literally in your physical body. This is where you will feel a pull. Or you will feel a resistance—a tightening. The sensations are subtle. However, with practice, you can get quite good at recognizing them. Then, proceed with whichever feels "right" and observe what happens next. What do you see? Whom do you interact with? How did it feel?

My favorite game to play in order to keep my connection to the download sharp is practicing finding the open parking spot in a crowded lot or street. Try it. Have fun.

The greater your sense of being stuck, the deeper you must look within yourself for answers. It is not enough to grow awareness of the actions and skills needed by reading, connecting to experts, and getting a mentor. Eventually, you must grow your awareness of what is happening inside you.

CHAPTER FIVE

GET CLARITY

THE SEARCH FOR CERTAINTY outside of our selfhood is a trap. I have faith in many things, from waking up tomorrow to the presence of the air I breathe. I am confident they are very likely to continue without interruption, indefinitely. Yet, they are not guaranteed. The only sure thing is what is within us.

If we learned nothing from the coronavirus pandemic, it is that unexpected chaos and disruption are always possible, waiting to ambush us around the next corner. They come with little or no warning and turn our world upside down. We are never immune to uncertainty—especially when it comes to our circumstances and relationships.

Back in 2008, I had a dream. At the time of the dream I was not yet engaged to my husband Barron, although we were dating seriously, and we were deeply in love with each other.

In the dream, I was the observer. I was watching Barron. My

dream self knew he would not live through the day. I was aware he knew his death was approaching too, and he accepted that outcome without any fear or regret. He went through his daily activities, just as if it were any other day, being fully present. He was comfortable with the life he had lived and had clarity about what he had come to do.

In the end of the dream, he was gone.

I gasped myself awake.

The meaning of the dream was absolutely clear to me—life was uncertain. We never know how much time we have, and I knew I didn't want to waste another day living as if I had eternity to be who I wanted to be and live as I wanted to live. Instead, I was clear that I wanted to spend all the minutes, days, and hours possible in Barron's company. I shared this dream and my insight with him, and four months later we were married.

Clarity is like that. It hits us, and, when we heed it, things shift very fast. But where exactly does it spring from, and how can we find it if it has been elusive?

THE SOURCE OF CLARITY–IT'S NOT WHAT YOU THINK

First, and foremost, clarity comes from within. Second, it arrives in its own way, at its own time. You cannot analyze or reason your way into it. It can appear on demand, but not always. That is why it is nonnegotiable that we work to build the connection to our intuition. Our inner wisdom will give us powerful direction, the more we open ourselves up to it, and the more we ask questions into it. When we establish that connection, clarity is more available to us.

Deciding to read this book is just one of an average thirty-five thousand decisions you and I each make every day. We try to make each decision be a good one—or, in other words, we want them to be effective, fulfilling, and, above all, right. We also try to make our decisions informed, rational, and smart.

But that's not how we actually decide most things. It is not how we decide whom we will love. It is not how we decide what is most important. No matter what life throws at us, we have the ability to adapt, learn, evolve, and grow. We can decide courageously and be unstoppable—no matter what happens next.

When we are not sure what to choose in a particular situation, we reach for information to help us. Usually that information is from other sources than our intuition. Unfortunately, when it comes to what we want, the search for data, research, and information won't provide effective direction. Data (often unverified or misrepresented) is more effective as a support for what we want or need instead of creating it. Social media is a well-known example of this practice of deciding on our stance, and then verifying what we have already decided by surrounding ourselves with others who echo the same ideas. That's not actually adding clarity or discernment. It is adding to our rigid stance.

Quite simply, no amount of information gives us clarity on our desires; quite the contrary. Information is so outrageously plentiful (and often conflicting) that it can overwhelm us, much like drinking from a fire hose. While information can show us what has happened or is likely to happen outside of us, it can never tell us what is transpiring inside of us.

The conflicting information we received during COVID-19 shows how elusive certainty can be when we crave it most. It also demonstrates clearly that we can decide entirely different things from the person next to us, even when the same info is available to us both.

When one major piece of our lives shifts, so do the facts and data. Facts are just temporary, based on context. This is a fundamental reason clarity can be so elusive, especially when we make facts into its foundation.

Truth, on the other hand, is universal and enduring. In other words, Truth (with a capital "T") is a principle, and it makes itself known to us when we have intuitive awareness. Truth principles include things like love, honesty, beauty, harmony, balance, peace, and joy; they often referred to as the attributes of God. It is those Truth principles we desire and search for more of in our lives.

Far from a useless philosophical idea, understanding our own Truth at this point, and being clear about it, is necessary in order to continue moving forward in our transformation. Why would we even consider making a change if there was not some Truth principle on the other side worth fighting for?

The challenge we inevitably face is getting clarity on what principle it is. When we are asked, "What is it you have that is worth fighting for?" as Wesley was asked in The Princess Bride, we aren't often confident enough to answer like he did: "True love." We fear making the wrong choice, and never recovering from the Pit of Despair he faced.

We could choose true peace. True joy. True beauty. True health. However, if we aren't clear which one is for us, we won't go far.

Even if the shift you have been struggling to make is a practical matter of trying to lose weight, or an urgent matter, such as getting out of an abusive relationship, principles like these must apply.

Step off the scale, or leave the house for a moment, so you can be by yourself—and then hear me on this: If you are stuck and have tried everything you can think of but nothing has worked, then you are likely focusing on the problem, not the principle. Moving forward is never about being rid of something. It is always about gaining something greater.

FIVE POWER QUESTIONS

There are five power questions that open up a world of possibility because they focus on solution—from the inside out. When you use them regularly, clarity is more readily available to you.

We are taught to consider problems first, and from the out-side in. The inside-out approach I am recommending is a 180-degree shift and is used by coaches and therapists. It acknowledges the problem, but instead of focusing on what is lacking, it moves directly into solution and what can be created.

As Albert Einstein famously said:

> *You can't solve a problem at the same level of thinking that created it.*

To reach a fresh level, you must access your own innate creativity and clarity. It will be important to address the following five paradigm-shifting questions. They are:

1. What do I want?
2. How does this align with my values?
3. What direction am I headed?
4. What obstacles exist?
5. How am I owning this decision?

What You Want

Our personal desires can be a messy mixture, to say the least. Some of our desires are what we believe we should desire in order to be responsible, good, or right. Then there are those desires that spring up from inside us. It can be difficult to untangle one from the other sometimes.

Asking yourself "What do I want?" is something we rarely do at all, much less with any depth. We assume we already know. Why ask?

The reason we must ask is that inner motivation is the only motivation we will go to any length to realize. It is also the only desire we have any ability to fulfill.

The answers we assume we know typically sound like "I want the economy to open up again," but that answer is still at the level of the problem. I don't have any measurable control over the economy, even when I vote for someone I think might fix it.

An answer I have more control over is "I want security and safety so I can thrive." This desire, besides being a basic human need, is also one that can be fulfilled by shifting our inner belief system and perspectives. It challenges us to think creatively and proactively—from the inside out.

I may not have control over the economy, but I absolutely can find ways to strengthen my ability to thrive, even in a sluggish or struggling economy.

Values: Our Soul's DNA

Our Truth lives in our principles. That's where we can look for clarity. The things that are of the greatest importance to us, and that we embody as our values, create what I call our "soul DNA."

We all have priorities and values. They are the foundation for our individual purpose and meaning. They are also the foundations for our true intentions. However, we don't usually stop to consider what they are. Doing so is going to help us navigate the obstacles we will face during a major shift. They become our guiding star.

Now that we have begun to build a connection with our inner guidance, we can get clear on what we value. Many times what we think we ought to value is not what we actually value, as demonstrated by our actions. It is extremely difficult to commit to a shift when there is a misalignment between what we say we want and our true, but contradictory, desire.

Your values are personal. But you don't really choose them. Rather, you recognize them. They become the measure that frames when a relationship or situation is right (or wrong) for you.

For instance, suppose you value respect, wisdom, adventure, and creativity above all things. You may find a work environment that is wildly creative, but you notice that there is an undercurrent of disrespect. If you know your values, you can easily recognize that this is not the right place for you, because the values are not aligned. You also know that this doesn't mean you must alter your values. Far from it. Without them you will be carried willy-nilly from one unfulfilling experience to the next with no inner direction.

If You Don't Know Where You Are Going, Any Road Will Do

When we are unclear what we are headed towards, we have a tendency to go in circles. In many uncomfortable situations we become obsessively worried about what we are headed away from and less about what we are headed towards. The missed opportunities in that negative skew are incredible.

When we focus on something we want to escape or be rid of, our view is distinctly negative. It places our attention on the problem instead of the solution. Even when we adamantly declare we want to be rid of it once and for all, we are still focusing on "it." The result is that precious energy required for exploring solutions and possibilities is used up on resisting.

One reason we choose to focus on where we have been, rather than where we are going, is we have the illusion that keeping an eye on it protects us from future harm. In fact, our choice to focus there—staring at it, discussing it endlessly, obsessing over it, and reinforcing its awfulness—only serves to strengthen its hold on us. In trying to exert power, we lose it.

Change happens first with us.

It is rarely—ever—motivating to move away from something. It is never motivating to repeatedly point at a problem, assigning blame, wallowing in all that is wrong. What excites us is solution. What excites us is vision. What excites us is the promise of growth, freedom, power, and passion.

That is the direction we must head. We can do this by envisioning ourselves feeling, acting, and experiencing what we will feel like when we arrive at where we are headed. Meditation is an excellent way to perform self-hypnosis and experience the bright future we are creating. This daydreaming approach has actually been shown to help us begin to embody the behaviors that will get us there faster and more effectively.

What matters is that we are moving towards a positive outcome and not running from a negative situation. Resistance of a situation or conflict with an individual is not solution. It holds your focus on the problem, which is negative, depleting—just like trying to do it all based on reason, holding a fifty-pound weight indefinitely.

Solution, by contrast, knows what it wants and moves towards that. So, for instance, instead of focusing on a debt situation, we can focus on how to grow income in new ways as so many businesses are doing now. Solution is innovative and creative when we recognize the situation and then take action to establish a fresh one.

Encountering Obstacles

The more important a shift is to us, the more likely we have already experienced obstacles—and will experience more.

Even when we are cruising along, like my husband's live entertainment booking agency in February of 2020, we can hit obstacles that are enough to devastate a thriving business. He was doubling in revenue year after year, but after COVID-19 hit, that dropped to a third of what it had been.

We can't always know what challenges are headed our way.

That's not the point.

Personally, I am one of those entrepreneurial types who leans into risk. I even seek them out. That's my approach to life. It isn't everyone's, and it doesn't need to be. But we all take risks every day. Getting behind the wheel of a car—especially in Atlanta, where I currently live—is a risk. It is a calculated risk.

Then there are risks we aren't even aware of that are headed our way—perhaps a pandemic, a natural disaster, or a loved one's catastrophic illness. We can never be fully prepared for how to handle that.

The important thing to know about risks is that we are always taking them, large and small. No shift is bulletproof. So consider what risks might stop or slow you down. When we think like that, we begin to recognize ways through and around those obstacles. The result is that in the face of unexpected obstacles we already have practiced adapting.

Risk demands it of us. Expect to adapt.

Acting As If

Until we commit to taking real, timely, measurable action on a shift, we aren't shifting. We are just daydreaming.

We can look at other people's action (or inaction) and wonder what possibly motivates them! It is always easier to see the blind spots of others, and certainly where they need to make a shift. We wonder why they don't just change, already! But we are all doing the best we can in this moment with the awareness and tools we have available to us. When we recognize the truth of every person's individual journey and perspective, we are better able to accept them as they are. Our own energy is best used working actively to change our own situation from where we currently are.

This, of course, implies that we must take action.

When it comes to taking action, I can be a poor judge of how long something is going to take. I also—as a business owner—can have countless balls in the air at once, which is definitely action—but it doesn't always translate into completion. If I don't write down the precise action steps I am going to take, when I will take them by, and either hold myself accountable or find someone who will hold me accountable, then I am likely to get distracted or overwhelmed. My shift is no shift at all.

I have a simple worksheet available on my website, at Stacey-RuthSays.com/ActionPlan, for writing down your own action steps to turn your decisions into action. It's free and simple to use. My Action Plan outlines your goals based on what you want, then addresses what action steps you can take to move towards your goal, what support could help you get there, and, then, holds your feet to the fire with a realistic timeframe and accountability.

Here are some exercises to help you confidently name your personal values.

EXERCISE FOR GREATER CLARITY:
THE VALUES WORKSHEET

On my website, StaceyRuthSays.com, you will find a free Values Worksheet, under Tools for Shift. There you will find some exercises to help you look at what it is you really value, and where you are "should-ing" all over yourself about what you think you ought to value. Without judging yourself—if you can do that—write down a list of things you spend most of your time doing. If it's shuttling the kids, surfing the internet, working three jobs—whatever it is, own it. This is your present reality. It doesn't have to define you.

It is, however, what you are currently valuing.

Below that is space to write in what you WANT to spend your time doing. It can be the same, but it is likely you will find differences.

The third section is where you can begin to write in words that are values. Here's where a lot of us trip over ourselves. We really value personal freedom, but we think we ought to value family and work—so we are out of alignment. We really value creativity and originality, but we think we ought to value a steady income—so we are out of alignment. Or the reverse can be true.

So take a few minutes now, and write down what you can. Then, if you have time now, I want you to write down the answers to the two very important questions at the bottom:

1. WHY do you want to do the things you want to?

2. WHY do you want to embody the values you do?

3. WHAT will the result be?

These questions challenge you to acknowledge the deep inner pull. This is your purpose calling you. Go big. Go deep. Lift your limiting ideas.

Get clarity.

CHAPTER SIX

OWN YOUR OWN SHIFT

ARE YOU READY FOR A SHIFT? Are you sure? When we shift we integrate two opposing dynamic forces. On one side we have our desire urging us forward. On the other is our fear pulling us back. Both are powerful. When we embrace them both and leverage the strength each contains, we are unstoppable.

We just explored the values and motivations that provide the necessary fuel for the fire of our inner desires. Without those being in the forefront of our minds, we are ripe for being overrun by our inner objections, doubts, and any misgivings.

When we are in alignment with our values and true desires, we are in a very exciting space, filled with possibility and promise. We can see our highest and best self more clearly. We can now see that the motivation and strength to make a meaningful shift comes from within us. It has been there all along.

There are really only three basic reasons to make a shift. What drives us is something we are seeking to create more of. Think of our values like gas in the car, while the three drivers are one of the following: greater freedom, power, or passion—or perhaps some combination of the three.

Along with each of these big three motivators comes a balancing influence that keeps our feet on the ground. It is like the mechanism that keeps us from turning the car off accidentally while driving or exiting the car if we haven't shifted into park first. It is extremely helpful to recognize each of the balancing influences, so we can integrate them fully for a more focused and effective shift.

REASON TO SHIFT:
FREEDOM VS. RESPONSIBILITY

The first reason to shift is the search for freedom. We are hungry to do things the way we want to. We are looking for freedom to do what we want, where we want, with whom we want, when we want. When we are free, we shake off the influence of others, finding a better, more creative, satisfying, and effective way.

Freedom feels incredible. This expression of our authentic self is powerful—and when we stuff it or allow someone else to block it (notice I said allow them, because it is always a choice) we become frustrated, resentful, or listless. We are not meant to be limited in our self-expression or how we live our lives.

But there is a balancing influence to freedom. That is the force of responsibility. It can bring us extreme stress. Fear of responsibility can keep us from shifting, at least at the level we long for. We've all heard the saying, "With freedom comes responsibility."

When I came down from the vortex in Sedona to start my first agency, I had a vision of strolling into my office each morning, as the sun streamed in the window, with a cup of coffee in hand, listening to some inspiring music and designing amazing, creative work until 5 PM. As I finished my fulfilling workday, I planned to make a delicious dinner and relax with a movie or a book. For the first time in years, I told myself, I would take the weekends off.

I anticipated the end to my twelve- and fourteen-hour days. My enslavement to high-pressure deadlines would be a thing of the past. Hours behind the wheel in bumper-to-bumper Atlanta traffic would become unnecessary.

That was my vision of freedom. However, it didn't address how to handle new responsibility as a business owner. As a result, my vision of freedom lasted about two weeks. My husband was very uneasy about me being a freelancer. He preferred his version of certainty and security, which meant a predictable paycheck. Today I know that idea of security is anything but certain. But then I didn't, and he wanted me to be earning—a lot. Immediately. I had responsibility to be part of our marital financial security, as I had agreed to be.

My start-up magazine client and coveted corporate client, Kimberly-Clark, along with several others, all had intense deadlines, and I was just one person. To keep them all happy, so they would pay me and I could satisfy my husband's concerns, as well as my own, I was in my office by 6:00 AM and worked until 11:00 PM. On weekends, I ran all over town to my printers, suppliers, client meetings, and client travel.

It was enough to suck the life out of my freedom fantasy—and fast. Although it felt awful at the time, responsibility is not actually a bad thing. It tempers our freedom in such a way that we build stronger freedom muscles. I had, in effect, turned over my freedom to my outside circumstances. So when the circumstances accelerated dramatically, I was completely unprepared and ungrounded. It was actually irresponsible to myself and undermined what was possible.

Responsibility, as a balancing influence, requires real clarity about what is, and what is not, ours to do. Because I had so much fear (stoked by my husband's fears) that there was not enough money coming in, and I was not good enough and had not yet built the strong connection to my inner source of freedom, I fell right back into what was familiar.

I did what I knew to do—which stretched me so thin, it broke that marriage apart and left me always rushing, missing deadlines, doing work I wasn't proud of, often sick, and always stressed.

When I struck out on my own a second time, starting Inside Out Marketing, I had learned a thing or two. I had done all the work I am sharing with you. Instead of rushing in, I started out fully self-funded for a year, allowing myself time to get established. I built relationships through networking, and when things didn't go the way I had planned (which inevitably happens to us all) I made adjustments. I invested in resources like accounting and in incredible productivity tools I didn't have access to back in 1997.

There were certainly times when I did slip into the old, familiar state of feeling overwhelmed during my start-up period. But when that happened, and when it happens now, I hit the pause button. I plan a day off to assess where I have overextended myself, and why. It is worth noting that this pause time actually requires tremendous self-restraint and self-responsibility, even today. At times I am most overwhelmed, I am least likely to believe I have the time to stop. However, it is the stopping that gives me back my freedom.

During one of these assessment days, I look at my values,

which I have written down and handy, along with my priorities. Am I in alignment with them?

I also examine my fears. What am I afraid of in this situation that I would back myself into a corner? Why would I limit my own Freedom? Am I taking on responsibilities that don't belong to me?

This line of questioning inevitably turns up some old fear about security or desire to be someone's savior. The first—security—is an illusion anyway, and is the number one inhibitor of our Freedom to be all we are meant to be. There is a reasonable balance, but it is grounded in faith and right action.

The second—trying to save someone—is actually a deep desire to prove value where I doubt myself. I tether my personal worth to whether I can fix, heal, promote, or otherwise improve another person. It might be an area where I am serving in a non-profit, or a client that is struggling to believe in themself fully. Wherever it rears up its head, I know I have over-burdened my own Freedom, dragging it down, I have also robbed the client of the crucial respect they gain from "rescuing" themselves. We each have the Responsibility to claim our own Freedom.

REASON TO SHIFT: POWER VS. VULNERABILITY

The second reason we are called to shift is a desire for power. Many of us have negative connotations around power, just like we do about money. But the reason we hold these views is because the idea of abuse of power is such a familiar theme in our world. Power is energy. It is strength. It is resiliency. It is our ability to create and to effect change.

When we are not the "decision maker" or the "authority" we can feel powerless. This makes us frustrated, resentful, and listless when those individuals in authority over us ask us to do things we can't do or we feel aren't right.

We often have zero power to change a client's mind or make leadership do things differently. We might wish we had the power to help our children do better in school or influence the next election. When we long for that sort of power we turn ourselves wrong side out trying to do things that are unrealistic or problematic. We may long to have the power of influence over others that seems to be missing, and we decide to initiate shift to get it.

There is a power we do have that is always available to us. Like freedom, it is inside us. That power is our attitude and our choice. We always have choices. Along with every choice there is also a consequence. Sometimes we don't care for that possible outcome.

As I slowly learned, if the choice I am making today isn't working for me—if it's negatively affecting my health, my pocket book, or my peace of mind—then it's time to make a different choice. The alternative is to play the victim. Victimhood is a role of pure powerlessness. It abdicates any responsibility we might have in creating a change for ourselves. Victimhood is a lie we tell ourselves.

It might not be comfortable at first, but to claim your self-respect, you absolutely must claim your power—not at someone else's expense, but for your own sake. Claiming your power, quite simply, means claiming your choices. Although you may not care for the potential consequence of your choice, this simple act is your superpower. Your frustration and resentment becomes enthusiasm and optimism, because you have become your very own, real-life hero, rescuing yourself from your self-made distress.

The other side of stepping into our power, is the balancing

force of vulnerability. When we claim our power, we cannot hide who we are. That means others will be looking at us. Celebrities and politicians are the most obvious examples of this. But so are CEOs and authors. So am I, right now, telling my experience and my truth. I am vulnerable every time I open my mouth and share my viewpoint on a stage, in a video, or in a blog. What will they think? Will they agree with me? Will they like me?

Social media, even when we share what we carefully curate for a perfect picture of ourselves, is a hugely vulnerable place to be. Bullying, shaming, unfriending, unfollowing—all these actions affect our sense of self-worth.

We are susceptible to the opinions of others because one of our most fundamental needs is to belong. There will always be those who agree and those who disagree with us. To make friends with vulnerability, we must know that our own personal worth (and our own personal power) exists entirely independent of what anyone else thinks, says, feels, or does.

Authentic truth always resonates, but not every truth resonates with everyone. Still, when we act out of our authentic truth, it is always collaborative. It is open. It is compassionate. It is empathetic. It is an expression of our inner strength. Vulnerability is the only route to power.

REASON TO SHIFT: PASSION VS. COMMITMENT

The third reason we shift is our passion. We can have many passions. Unlike our individual purpose, passion is about emotions that drive us. Our passion inspires us and is built on what makes us feel good. Purpose is the reason, or the "why" behind what we do, primarily as a contribution to the world.

In exercise 2 of the introduction, "Get Clear about Your Passions," we explored the deep connection between our passions and our connection to joy.

Finding your passion is really just about what lights you up and gives you joy—or at least a deep sense of satisfaction. It does not need to be what you do to earn income—although it can be. For instance, I am passionate about hiking the many trails around our home, and I have a bucket list item of hiking the Camino del Santiago in Spain. Nonetheless, I don't intend to become a travel blogger. Another passion I have is animal rights and promoting the ethical treatment of animals. I happen to believe how we treat animals directly affects how we treat one another. However, again, I am not planning to become a paid activist or a veterinarian.

Passions tend to be the places where you lose your sense of time passing, or you daydream about doing more of it. Passions are where you are compelled to show up, engage, and nurture something. Often, however, we amputate ourselves from our passions at some point, because we felt (or someone told us) they were foolish, unrealistic, or interfered with what was really important.

If this feels like it might be your story, spend some time journaling about what you loved to do as a child, regardless of how the inner critic might try to interfere in the same voice that told us it was foolish or unrealistic. If you loved chasing fireflies, put it down. You don't have to make sense of it. Just acknowledge it. And perhaps go chase some fireflies tonight.

People are increasingly looking to their work to be the source of their joy. Who has not heard the phrase "do what you love and the money will follow"? That is actually a pretty recent concept, which is an incomplete and narrow view of the role of our passions. Globally, men and women derive a majority of their sense of self-worth and accomplishment from their work when there is so much more to life. Our language and norms reflect this. When we meet someone, the first thing we tend to ask is—"What do you DO?"

I work with many individuals who feel they are failing because they are unfulfilled in their work, or they are doing the work they are passionate about, but it isn't providing a reasonable income. Now— don't get me wrong—I absolutely believe there are those who find a passion that also provides good income. However, if the two don't coincide, it doesn't cancel the validity of your passion—or the necessity of earning an income.

Sometimes work is just work. And our passions are our passions, independent of our paycheck. Our passions don't need financial income to validate them.

This is where the third balancing force comes into play. The other side of our passion is our commitment. It's true in relationships, and it's true in our work. When I speak about being an unstoppable leader, I ask, "What if your work was so inspiring that it felt effortless"? I believe that is absolutely possible for anyone and everyone. But effortless doesn't mean you take a passive role and everything just happens for you. You are actively committed when you are leading.

Effortless means not resisting. It means releasing the struggle. The judgment. Perfectionism.

Let me explain.

When you are passionate about something, you are willing to pour your time and energy into it. You can focus on it and lose track of time. You don't expect to be perfect at it right out of the gate. The process of doing it is your satisfaction. Whether you are learning a musical instrument or a new language; building muscle, a wardrobe or a house; or being a top sales person, a CEO, or a coach—expect to make a commitment. You are committing to the process. You are committing to yourself to see it through.

Commitment isn't a burden. It is 100 percent necessary to move you forward. Without commitment, we have passion with no action. Commitment is willing to take risk—and if there are challenges, commitment is flexible, resilient, and hopeful. Commitment looks for solution without blame or shame. Commitment is willing to be wrong and try a different approach. It isn't attached to how we reach our destination. It keeps going via an alternate route as needed.

What does this look like?

Well, commitment is the forty-eight-year-old woman who has had a lifelong dream of being a photographer but who works part-time as a teacher's assistant to pay the bills while freelancing and growing her photography business.

Commitment is the speaker and author who provides marketing strategy while she's building her speaking and writing career.

These individuals are passionate about what they are doing, and they are committed to do what is needed to get there.

When we can see the forces that are pulling us forward, and at the same time acknowledge those that hold us back, we can see the gifts in all of it. We can see ourselves in all of it. The truth is, to own our own shift, we cannot shift only a piece of ourselves. When we shift, we must shift our whole self. To own our own shift, we must allow our shift to own us.

WALKING THE WALK

I am one of two million people around the world who have done a fire walk. Some of you may have had that experience as well. Talk about feeling the fear and doing it anyway! I like to try things and have grand adventures. So when I was invited to a retreat that was planning a fire walk on the first night, I really wanted to try it.

I had heard fire walking required some sort of mind over matter trancelike mindset, and I really wasn't sure I had what it took to mentally override the laws of physics. So I did what anyone in my position would do—I Googled it. I knew there had to be a physical explanation for how fire walks work. I was right.

The science of fire walks is fascinating. The fire is burned down to coals and embers, and while the coals, which are on top, don't conduct heat, the embers, on the bottom, do. The trick is to not dawdle, or stand still, so your weight doesn't cause you to sink into the embers. It is equally important not to run or race across the fire, which also puts weight on the balls of your feet, pushing the embers up between your toes. Just take a nice stroll at a moderate pace across the coals and you are all good.

Or so I thought.

When I arrived, I learned there's a lot of ritual to fire walks. Some ritual is old and spiritual, like naming the thing we want to invite into our life, writing it on a piece of paper, and then naming the thing we want to let go in order to make space for what we are calling forth, and writing that down. Then there are some newer rituals, like signing a legal waiver, and watching a PowerPoint about the fire walk horror stories of those who wound up in the emergency room.

After all of that, there were about eighty of us that night who helped build the fire, blessed the fire, and placed the papers with the things we wanted to let go of into the fire. We sang a simple, uplifting song as, one by one, about thirty of us walked up to the fire.

The heat of a fire walk is incredible. Nine feet of hot coals are in front of you. Eighty people are watching you. The facilitator is standing at the other end of the coals, with the piece of paper containing what you want most to achieve, saying, "Come get it," ready to catch you when you make it across.

You can feel the emotion.

And the fear.

And the desire.

All that Google science goes right out the window.

When you are standing on the edge of the fire, what you have to ask yourself is, "Is this mine to do?"

Do I have it in me to walk on fire?" For me, the answer was "Yes." That doesn't mean my answer would always be yes—or that those who didn't walk on fire that night were any lesser because they didn't. It just wasn't theirs to do. They held space, and sang and cheered on those of us who did.

I would do it again. In fact, in many ways I do it every day. Those flames are just like the challenges that come up in my life— my work—my marriage—every day. I helped to build them. I helped to bless them. I choose to walk through them.

My mind will tell me that this is doable and countless people have done this successfully before me. Still, my feelings and beliefs can get in my way and hold me back, especially if I am not aware of them. They can stop me if I let them. But I want to be unstoppable. I want to walk across my personal shift like a badass.

WHAT IS YOURS TO DO?

The question to ask yourself is this: What is mine to do?

We've all got the fire in us. It calls us. It is always urging us to act, whether it is for the sake of freedom, power, or passion. That fire within us gives us joy. It is where we are fascinated, inspired, curious, or where our attention is led over and over again. It helps us be all we are meant to be. Our inner fire is worth walking across real, live fire for. It is the purpose behind our shift.

EXERCISES TO OWN YOUR SHIFT

Exercise 1: What Is Mine to Do?

What is calling you?

What is tugging at the edges of your awareness?

Think about this question.

What is it that you picked up this book longing to do?

This is yours.

It might seem impossible, or a little foolish, or the "how" might be unclear—but, nonetheless, it is calling you.

You are ready.

You get to name and claim what you want. We tend to get really hung up on thinking there must be this one thing. In fact, there can be lots of things. You can pick one for now. Pick the big one and the one that comes up first, without you analyzing it.

Right now, we are not going to focus on how you are going do it. We are listening to your deepest desires without judging or qualifying them—and oh, boy! Don't we love to judge and qualify them!

Without trying to figure out how, just be aware of the desire. Then write it down. Now, hold onto that. That is where your shift is going to happen. That is where you are meant to be unstoppable.

First, of course, you must be aware of it. Then you must act on it by moving toward it. You get to embody it. Little by little or by great leaps and bounds. But you must inevitably take action.

You can write it here:

_____

_____

_____

_____

_____

Exercise 2: What Is Stopping Me?

So look at that desire you wrote down. Let me ask you, if you aren't actively fulfilling that desire right now and shifting so it becomes your reality—what's stopping you?

We are taught to look at our circumstances. We say— oh, it's my finances. Or, my responsibilities are overwhelming. My car is broken. I'm sick. The kids, or my aging parents, have to come first. I don't have the right education or skill set. I just don't have enough money to do what I want. Or we might blame our boss, our company, or "the establishment"—"they" won't allow me to do what I want. Then there's the market—there's so much competition. It is impossible to stand out. It goes on and on and on.

Even so, look at that "thing" you just wrote down a little while ago. That's the thing waiting for you at the other end of the fire walk. This is your inner desire talking to you. You would walk across fire for this. Now, what is really stopping you?

It isn't your circumstances.

Not really.

It's your fear. Nothing else. What are you afraid of losing—or not being able to get? Now answer these questions as honestly as you are able:

1. Is there a person or situation I want to escape? Why? What's the fear?

2. Do I find myself in an uncomfortable or disappointing repeating pattern of relationship, situation, or behavior that I don't know how to avoid? Why? What's the fear?

3. What is changing in my life that I am currently resisting? Why might I be resisting this change?

4. Is there something I am afraid of with respect to this change?

5. What am I afraid may happen to me if I allow this change?

6. What is the payoff for keeping things the way they are?

7. What's the cost of keeping things the way they are?

When you can name a fear, you can release it. You can bless the place in you that was afraid. It needs your love. It needs you to tell it you have got this, baby!

You don't need to make this fear your reality. You get to choose a new reality, right now.

Let the fear go. Write it down. Get it out. Don't be afraid of the fear any more.

You can write it here:

_____

_____

_____

_____

_____

_____

_____

CHAPTER SEVEN

INITIATION

TAKE A MOMENT AND BREATHE. Look how far you have come! Now that you have even a smidge of clarity about who you are, and what has stopped you, it is like seeing the world with fresh eyes. I made you stretch a little, but it wasn't that bad, was it? You don't have all the answers yet, but you probably feel more awake. Your perspective has shifted. Perhaps things your mentor said earlier suddenly start to make sense—especially the things you were resisting. At this point, if you have been doing the exercises, you have renewed hope and energy. You may even believe you have arrived, and you wonder what is left to do.

You are likely to begin to see some transformation happening for you, and it feels good. It might even feel fantastic! You've lost some weight (just a pound or two!), or you are paying off the debt a few dollars at a time where before you were barely treading water.

You are learning how to stand up for yourself without being defensive, and, to your amazement, people are more respectful of your ideas. You are making time to be creative, or you are learning a new skill. The point is: your shift has already begun. You are stepping into your power, passion, and freedom now.

This is a stage that you will revisit again . . . and again. It is an elevated sense of consciousness and requires cultivation. It comes with a warning on the label though:

You are unlikely to maintain this state 24/7, and if you become too attached to it, when you lose it temporarily, you might tend to think it is gone forever and that you have failed, which tempts you to give up. Do not discontinue use without checking with your mentor first! They can share their own experience of losing ground before they gained even more.

Never lose sight of the fact that you got here once—you can do it again.

WALK THIS RICE PAPER

In the 1970s television series *Kung Fu*, Master Kwan tells monastic initiate Kwai Chang Caine that when he could finally walk a whisper-thin sheet of rice paper and leave no trace, he would have learned. He would have become a true Shaolin monk.

The intensive learning Caine underwent is key in any initiation. We are in the midst of a rite of passage for ourselves at this point. Whatever we were holding onto in the hallway has already lost some of its appeal. Walking our own personal rice paper becomes our focus as we discover a new way of being.

As initiates, we are now immersed in a new set of activities or skills. We will most likely do them poorly at first, just like Kwai

Chang. He tried for ten years before he was able to successfully walk that rice paper. You probably won't need to work at it that long, though, so don't freak out!

Whatever new activities you are undertaking in your shift, you are sure to take a tumble here and there. It's part of this awkward learning stage. There will be frustration and a sense of "I'll never be any good at this!"—which is usually right before the breakthrough. So hang in there.

The most important thing any of us need at this point is a Master Kwan. Their perspective is golden. The master shows us the objective clearly and steadily feeds us the practices we need to achieve it, at a pace we can handle. They also provide reassurance that any fumbles and stumbles are normal for all of us. They reflect back to us how far we have come already, reminding us of where we were just a short while ago. Lastly, they hold us accountable for doing the work required for sustainable change.

THE PINK CLOUD EFFECT

A little euphoria is good for you. That's what happens when we are in the early stages of our breakthrough. We start feeling better. We have obtained these amazing insights and aha moments.

In fact, when you reach this point in the shift process, it is exactly like falling in love! The physical effects mirror drug addiction. We are, quite literally, on a natural high. Our body's own chemicals that cause this euphoria—adrenaline, dopamine, oxytocin, and vasopressin—are all released. Dopamine, especially, creates elation and energy around whatever new activity we are now doing—just like a new love.

What's more, your inhibitions drop as a result of oxytocin (known as the "love drug") in your body. Like alcohol, oxytocin reduces anxiety and fear—making you more boastful, confident, and willing to do what felt too risky or vulnerable before.

Since it is limiting beliefs that have held us back—ones that we felt insulated us from unbearable vulnerability—this chemical shift provides just enough space for us to have a fresh experience despite ourselves.

During this phase we feel almost superhuman. Our brain begins to light up as we do the things that we now associate with our shift. We are happier, and we associate all this feel-good energy with the changes we are making.

All of the body's natural euphoric response is tremendously helpful. It is so powerful that it jump-starts the rewiring of your brain, creating those new grooves that result in positive new thought patterns. It is much, much harder to change if you can't get this "love" hit of the pink cloud. In fact, you are more likely to abandon your shift if you don't.

It is only natural that we want to share this new experience with everyone around us. We share the feelings, the wins, and the details of our process so far. Often we even actively recruit our friends and family members to join us and become a part of our tribe—with mixed response. Some are envious, while others do join us. Some could care less and wish we would just keep it to ourselves.

I absolutely encourage this intense desire to share. When we do, we get this wonderful payoff of accelerated rewiring of our brain. The more we share, the deeper the groove. However, don't get too attached to others' responses for further motivation. If you do, negative feedback, especially if you are looking for validation, can undo your progress.

WHY MUST THIS FEELING END?

The pink cloud, like infatuation, is only temporary. It gets us over a really big hurdle and blocks some pain of transformation. That is its purpose. But it isn't built to last.

Research has uncovered that during romantic infatuation it is impossible for us to create real emotional intimacy. We're too physically amped. So, even though it feels pretty incredible, there is something more enduring and fulfilling on the other side.

The pink cloud must end in order for us to get to the prize. While it reinforces our shaky new behaviors, it also blocks the lasting shift until it dissipates. Hard as that may be to believe, you actually want your excitement to ultimately settle down.

THE POINT OF NO RETURN

There is actually no point of no return, although it can feel like it. Real shift never demands eternal commitment. It simply cannot. You can make a new choice—even choosing to return to the hallway—whenever it feels right, because shift won't work when it is imposed on you. You either enter into it willingly, or you fizzle out pretty fast.

When the initial buzz of initiation wears off, and you are left with just you and those awkward new behaviors, you may find what excited you at first now makes your skin crawl. This happens in new relationships, recovery, fitness, business, and every other big, meaningful shift. Each of these can create an uncomfortable new reality when the excitement dies. At this point you see things as they really are. The new love steps down off the pedestal of perfection that infatuation created, and you realize they are a neat freak, can't balance their checkbook, or are overly sensitive in a certain area.

The great part about this awareness is that it happens after you have had a small taste of what the other side of shift looks like. With all their imperfect behaviors, this person cherishes you and makes you feel seen and heard. Now you have a fair comparison of your before and after. Is the freedom to be messy more important than being cherished? Good question! The information you have gathered up to this point about what freedom might be like, should you choose to stick it out, helps you discern: Is it worth it?

Only you can answer that question. This is why you need some awareness of your values and connection to your intuition. If you are questioning if this was really the right direction for you, then check in with your intuition, and revisit those values.

Does this still feel right?

Should you make some adjustments?

And, of course, you don't have to decide in a vacuum. Your mentor and your tribe are great sounding boards. They can share what happened for them when they reached this point of uncertainty.

A really good mentor won't push you to stuff your inner conflict, suck it up, and get on with it. Instead they will join you in asking the right questions to get better clarity. They will definitely call you on any rationalizations your ego might be making to avoid change. Unfortunately, we generally are stubbornly resistant when our thinking is challenged. That is why challenging us is the most important role of a mentor.

Ultimately, the point of no return is an infinite loop, where you get to keep choosing and rechoosing to stay the course—or not. There is really no greater freedom or power than realizing we always have choices, and we get to take the responsibility for making them.

THE EGO AND THE INITIATE

Our ego is likely to be highly agitated during the initiation phase. It has a natural role in our psyche and is not the villain it is often portrayed to be. Still, ego can be a seductive destroyer of self-transformation, and the more we understand what naturally happens to our ego during shift, the better we can navigate it.

Our ego's number one job is protecting us from harmful change. The only problem is that it cannot discern the difference between harmful and healthy change. So it just blocks any and all change where we let it.

Ego is the seat of our personalities and designed to maintain a strong sense of personal identity—and healthy self-esteem.

"The self-consciousness system is the narrating part of human consciousness that reflects on one's thoughts, feelings and actions and inhibits or legitimizes them to one's self and to others. In this sense, ego is very like what is meant by the term identity, and ego functioning refers to the components of the self-consciousness system that relate directly to mental health" (Gregg Henriques, PhD, "The Elements of Ego Functioning," blog, PsychologyToday.com, June 27, 2013).

When our ego is healthy, it:

- Is reflective, responsive, and resourceful

- Thinks in terms of possibilities

- Is optimistic and grateful

- Is curious

- Does not personalize what others say or do; maintains a healthy perspective

- Embraces the imperfections of self, others, and life
- Takes ownership of problems; lets other people handle themselves
- Practices acceptance, compassion, and cooperation
- Acts with integrity and authenticity
- Can discern between what can and cannot be changed
- Has a strong sense of personal power
- Is adaptive and flexible
- Feels worthy
- Can give and receive love and appreciation
- Is aware of interests, desires and talents (Caroline deBraganza, "Stop Demonizing Ego. It's Not What You Think," blog, medium.com/change-your-mind/stop-demonising-ego-its-not-what-you-think-699ee6200f6, November 24, 2018).

However, an unhealthy ego is the ego most people refer to, and it:

- Feels inadequate
- Refuses to face fears and challenges
- Expects perfection
- Uses blame, avoidance, criticism, or denial in difficult situations
- Feels a sense of entitlement or grandiosity
- Competes with others (I'm better/worse than you)
- Is jealous or judgmental of other's success

- Avoids making apologies and taking responsibility

- Needs to be right and feel superior (deBraganza, "Stop Demonizing Ego.")

When we find ourselves struggling to shift, our ego needs some healing. In easier shifts we have little resistance from our ego. We are egoically in a healthy relationship with that area of our life. But in a challenging shift we face an ego that feels its life is being threatened, because it is not healthy.

Most of what we perceive as obstacles as we shift are merely creations of our ego, on a subconscious level, built to prevent us from changing. The intention is to prevent us from feeling inadequate, anxious, or unsure, which equate to "death" for our ego.

This is why your book, or your work of the heart, is so difficult to finish. It's why you have the logo and website for your new business, but you haven't approached your first client yet. It's why those problems you thought were solved by leaving your last relationship followed you into this one.

Happily, we are not doomed to being cellmates with this damaged ego forever. Carl Jung proposed that the purpose of life is shifting from ego-consciousness to the self through individuation. The self, Jung references, desires to create and evolve. That's the reason we are here—to evolve, or shift. However, the damaged ego prefers the illusion of safety with things just the way they are. In other words, a damaged ego creates a metaphorical death for us that is potentially worse (stagnation) than the metaphorical death (loss or failure) it is trying to protect us from.

If you're unhappy with your habits, self-image, or your current life, your ego is likely the culprit. Still, we owe it some gratitude. As children, it helped us develop coping mechanisms to deal with an unfamiliar, overwhelming world. Now, as adults, we have a clearer sense of self and the ability to perceive reality without feeling threatened.

As initiates, we have begun to see reality for what it is, instead of the way our ego has whispered it is. We are not as frightened or easily intimidated. We have had a taste of the power, passion, and freedom within the self.

A damaged ego is going to tell us we don't deserve that, or we aren't enough to maintain it. It will distract us with old habits and thought patterns. Our job isn't to shut the ego down or make it wrong, but to be aware of what is happening. We now know what the characteristics of a healthy ego are, and we get to use them to heal the unhealthy ego's influence. I will show you how.

A willingness to shift is a willingness to heal the parts of our ego that have been wounded. As a result, we become more whole. That's real power, and it is heady stuff.

EXERCISE TO BEGIN HEALING THE EGO

Exercise 1: Meet Your Higher Self

Within each of us there is an essential, wise, true, "higher self" that is untainted by whatever life has thrown at us. This higher self is simply another aspect of ourselves that we fail to regularly tap into, much like our intuition. Many believe this self is actually a personification of our intuition, while others believe it is a channel for our spirit guides and angels, and some say it is our soul itself. Regardless, this self is timeless and ageless, and far more powerful than our ego. Even so, our ego strives to protect it, when such an idea is more like an ant racing around trying to protect an elephant.

This exercise is a self-guided meditation to still the ego, bring the higher self forward into our consciousness, and show both us and our ego the real power we have at our disposal. Since it is a meditation, I encourage you to record yourself reading it aloud, and then play it back, so you can have the full experience.

Meditation: Get into a relaxed posture, either seated in a chair or lying down. Keep your back straight, shoulders relaxed, and feet flat on the floor. Make certain there are no distractions, and place your palms facing up gently on your lap if you are sitting and on the surface beside you if you are lying down.

Now, as you relax fully, breathe deeply—inhaling and exhaling for three deep breaths. As you take that first breath in, filling your lungs without straining or tension, say silently to yourself, "I am."

Now, holding your breath on the inhale for three beats, and as you exhale, mentally think the phrase, "Letting go."

Inhale deeply again, thinking the phrase in your mind, "I am."

Hold for three beats.

Now exhale, as you mentally repeat the phrase, "Letting go."

One more time now. Inhale deeply, with the phrase, "I am." Hold for three beats, and exhale with the phrase, "Letting go."

That's good. Now let your breath relax. Let your

thoughts move through your mind like clouds through the sky without paying any attention to them. Just let them drift in and out of your awareness. It is so peaceful here. You have let everything go and are just drifting in this place.

In this gentle, safe space, begin to move your awareness to a very comfortable and quiet place out in nature. It might be a brook, forest, meadow, garden, mountain, or ocean. Wherever you feel drawn.

Look around at your sacred place and notice how peaceful it is here.

Listen to the sounds of the birds and breeze around you and recognize how calm and tranquil it is.

Smell the air and become aware of the oxygen and of natural scents.

Feel the earth beneath your feet and the air on your face. Perhaps reach out and touch a plant, stone, or water.

Now feel the warmth of the sun on your face. You are comfortable, relaxed, and peaceful here.

As you soak in these sensations you can sense that you are not alone in this place. A loving presence is here, offering you support and guidance. It takes on whatever form is most comforting and reassuring to you. It tells you that it recognizes your worth and loves you and accepts you completely.

It has been with you since the beginning of time. This loving presence wants only your highest and best good. Whatever you desire, this being—your highest self—also desires for you as well.

You higher self wants to give you gifts. Open your heart to receive them.

First it places a brilliant purple jewel in your open palm.

It shimmers in the sun and sparkles. Your higher self tells you, "This is your inner wisdom and deep intuitive knowing."

Accept this jewel, and thank your higher self. Promise to keep this jewel with you always.

Next your higher self places a beautiful, multifaceted jewel that changes color into your other palm. Feel its weight in your hand. Sometimes it seems pink and then as it catches the light it appears green. Your higher self tells you, "This is perfect love and compassion."

Accept this jewel as well, and again, give thanks to your higher self for these treasures. Promise to carry this gift with you always as well.

You higher self receives your thanks.

Now, you higher self wants to know what questions you have brought as gifts for them. Quietly consider what questions are on your heart. Know it is always a gift to give these questions to your higher self. They are precious because they are yours, and they matter to you deeply.

Offer your questions. Describe your needs and your concerns. Each one is another shimmering jewel that falls from your lips.

As your higher self catches each one, listen for the responses. You may hear them speak words or their answers may come in other ways, gestures, symbols, or sounds. Thoughts may enter your mind or feelings and sensations may occur in your body.

Your higher self may respond to your questions in many different ways, so listen for these responses and whatever ways they come to you, without expectation. As you do, know that you are in a space that allows you to easily absorb the directions and the support your higher self has for you.

Remain open to receiving any and all answers that come to you.

As you listen, go deeper in your questions. Ask you higher self:

What do I need to do next to fulfill this shift in my life?

[PAUSE—allow some space for an answer to be felt.]

What limited beliefs do I need to release to shift easily and effortlessly?

[PAUSE—allow some space for an answer to be felt.]

What else do I need to let go of to move forward and really make a shift?

[PAUSE—allow some space for an answer to be felt.]

How can I know that I am always supported in my shift I am undertaking?

[PAUSE—allow some space for an answer to be felt.]

How can I tune into your guidance during my daily experiences as I shift?

[PAUSE—allow some space for an answer to be felt.]

What is the best course of direction I can take in order to make this shift I desire?

[PAUSE—allow some space for an answer to be felt.]

What sign can I anticipate to know that I am moving in the right direction?

[PAUSE—allow some space for an answer to be felt.]

What else do I need to know about my path?

[PAUSE—allow some space for an answer to be felt.]

Take a deep breath in and realize that if you didn't receive a direct answer to your questions, you will in the hours days and weeks ahead.

At this moment you notice that your higher self is holding a beautiful box, in which is another a gift for you. You can hardly believe it. As you open the box and receive your gift, you see it is something you can use in the future to help you easily return to this sacred place to meet with your higher self—your own special gift that you can use to transport yourself to this place of inner guidance whenever you choose. Look at what is in the box. It has meaning to you. Whatever it is and whatever form it takes is whatever you see it to be. Whenever you meditate on this gift, you will be able to return to this place and connect with your higher self.

Now thank your higher self for all the answers and the gifts you have received, for meeting with you in this special, sacred space. Returning to the present moment, and to your breath, bringing your gifts with you, feel more of your life energy moving through your body. Feel mentally, physically, spiritually, and emotionally rejuvenated. The nature scene recedes as you sense yourself moving into your full potential as the powerful creator you are.

And so it is. You can open your eyes. Take a few moments to reconnect to where you are, wiggle your fingers and toes, focus your vision, and then write down any answers that came up for you during this meditation.

Exercise 2: Affirmations

Affirmations are extremely healing for our psyche—and our ego. They provide both reassurance and a new idea to focus on.

Below are my all-time favorite affirmations, covering a variety of common limiting beliefs. I am sharing them with you, and if they resonate with a particular situation you are experiencing, write them down, and place them where you will see the affirmation regularly. Repeat the affirmation any time the situation or thought crosses your mind, so you are infusing your neural pathways with a new idea at least as often as the old idea.

It is a good practice to speak the affirmation aloud, especially in the evening before bed and first thing in the morning. These are the times your subconscious mind is most open to suggestion and can receive the greatest benefit.

Affirmations for Transforming Negativity into Positivity:

- I am a child of God, and a person of worth, who deserves to be happy, joyous, and free.

- Even though (situation you are experiencing, e.g., I am lonely or work is exhausting), I love and approve of myself completely.

- I listen to my body. It knows what it needs.

- I am confident in who I am and my abilities.

- I am open to guidance, and am constantly receiving good, orderly direction.

- I trust in my inner desires.

- I am loved. I am strong. I am enough.

- Life is happening for me—not to me.

- I am worthy of love, and I am loving.

- I matter. I am here to do great things.

- I am open to positive opportunities and surprises today.

- I am at peace and trust the process happening in my life.

- I radiate love and kindness, and that is reflected back to me.
- I am happy and I inspire others to be as well.
- I communicate clearly what I need to others.
- Success and abundance come naturally to me.
- I am fully present and confident in my future.
- I can accomplish anything I set my mind to.
- I am aware of my emotions and can let them go without getting attached to them.
- Every part of me vibrates with energy and health.

CHAPTER EIGHT

PLAN TO PRACTICE

PLAN TO PPRACTICE IS THE ROUTE TO MASTERY, and the only way to practice something is to do it. Then we must do it again. Making a difficult shift is just like learning to walk, or tie your shoes, drive a car, nurture a relationship, or solve an equation for X. It takes repetition and committed action, until it becomes a part of us and we can even do it by rote. The metaphysical Law of Action states:

> *We must act on our intentions,*
> *since the law can only work through us.*

Of course, that is not where we begin. Whenever you are tempted, in that ego voice, to beat yourself up for not having mastered this stuff yet, gently remind yourself that you definitely learned to walk, and you can do this too—if you keep at it.

READY, FIRE, AIM

Practice without a plan is like trying to hit a target blindfolded. It is possible you might hit it, but your ability to repeat your random success is marginal. That's the "ready, fire, aim" approach. Aiming first is proven to be a more reliable approach. A plan focuses your efforts for maximum impact.

Poor planning is the result of most business failures, personal budget overruns, and disaster management debacles. Your current shift is no different. Happily for you, your plan doesn't need to be complex or rigid. You just need one.

A plan by definition is making a decision to do something in advance of doing it. You are setting intentions for what actions you will take. That's all. Just look at what you can do to move towards your objective, and then settle on what micro-step you can do now. It really is that simple—which can be baffling.

I am including a small exercise at the end of this chapter to get you going on your plan, or you can work with your guide to develop one. Generally, your plan will contain a flexible set of activities that can be incorporated into your routine without overwhelming you. Most spiritual practices include a daily reading and meditation and/or prayer time, which can be as little as five minutes in the beginning. Fitness practices gradually introduce modest cardio and strength with only a few repetitions.

Part of my plan for nurturing my marriage today is to ask and answer four questions with Barron at the dinner table almost every night. The process takes us about five to ten minutes, and we learn more about ourselves while connecting with each other in a very intimate way. The questions are:

1. What made you smile today?

2. What tested you today?

3. What are you looking forward to?

4. What are you afraid of right now, and how can I help?

Because this is part of our plan for keeping our marriage strong, we have come to expect and even prepare for it throughout the day. Sometimes our answers are funny, while at other times they are raw and lead to deeper discussion. This is an enormous shift for me, given my past marriage experience. It is a core, healing practice for both of us.

On rare occasions one of us is so distracted or distraught from the day that we ask for a pass on the evening's session. That is part of the plan, because, even though we generally enjoy it, it requires a level of centeredness on both our parts to be fully present.

Having a plan provides structure to our intentions. In my marriage my intention is to cultivate intimacy between us and support one another on a daily basis so we can be more of who we are individually. We are devoted to each other's evolution—together. Barron shares this intention. We have a purpose for our life together, and our plan makes it a reality.

A flexible plan adapts to the fluctuations of life—so long as we don't depart from the plan more often than we adhere to it. If we abandon our plan repeatedly, then it is not really an effective plan. If this happens, it is time to look once again at whether we are moving in the right direction and, if so, devise a better plan that is better suited to both our personality and our desires.

DON'T JUST DO SOMETHING. SIT THERE

Many of us try to move into the action of practice immediately after we become sick and tired of our current reality. Unfortunately it is unlikely for actions to make a meaningful difference if they are not done with clarity and guidance.

The rush into practice is a common response to our heightened discomfort, and we will explore that more in the next chapter. What is important to know right now is that shift is a process, and process takes patience, persistence, and willingness.

So be certain before you build your plan that you do, in fact, know what has been stopping you, and where you are headed, with the right support and guidance in place. My husband and I both have spiritual guides and relationship guides who help us navigate the occasionally tumultuous waters known as "marriage." I occasionally wonder if my first marriage would have endured had Mark and I had the wonderful resources Barron and I have now.

Being fully present in our practice when we are doing it is absolutely essential. Listen for the inner dialog, which might include resistance, distraction, pain, insight, or wonder and delight at your own power and resiliency. If at all possible, observe yourself during your practice, as a nonjudgmental witness. Observe your body. Observe your breath, pulse, and areas where you are tight or sore. Observe your thoughts and emotions during your activity. This is also a key principle of mindfulness and extremely helpful when we are altering a pattern of behavior.

If you can be observant and curious as you are doing these new actions, rather than becoming obsessively goal-oriented, you are likely to have a more pleasant experience, first. Second, you will activate that powerful 90 percent of your brain that contains your creativity, inspiration, and intuitive guidance. That Goliath within you will provide the resources to keep going, and heal your wounded ego. Give it free reign.

When we become goal-oriented, we move into the more restrictive 10 percent of our brain. We literally contract. We are constantly judging and monitoring our efforts. It is like we become the child in the back seat on a long road trip, impatiently asking, "Are we there yet? Are we there yet?"

In truth, you are in the driver seat, and you know you are going to arrive in due time, but we have to go the distance required, and it is much more pleasant when everyone can just relax and enjoy the scenery. So, even while you are practicing and taking action, do it with as much presence and awareness as you can muster.

You have come so far already. Stay the course. All the deep work you have done, clarity you have gained, and consciousness you have acquired are a solid foundation. However, you must put it all into action.

Every shift requires a plan; it requires daily commitment to practice. If you aren't willing to take action or to do the inner work, that is just good information. Explore if you may have moved in a direction that wasn't quite aligned with your values and priorities. If not, that's just another opportunity to stay connected to the inner guidance and adjust your course.

Allow whatever you learn about yourself to be okay, and revisit your shift again when you are ready. Otherwise, it is time for a change, with a clear set of actions.

GIVE IT AWAY

The Bible contains many perplexing statements, one of the most perplexing of which is Matthew 25:29—"For whoever has will be given more, and they will have an abundance. Whoever does not have, even what they have will be taken from them." (NIV).

That just doesn't seem very fair, now does it? It is more like those riddles we studied to open up our intuition. The one who already has something in this passage doesn't have material wealth, of course. What they have is faith. They have belief and understanding. Those are the underpinnings of this shift you are embarking on. The more belief you have—in yourself—and that real shift is possible—the more momentum you develop, and the stronger that belief becomes. When you wallow in self-doubt and negativity, the more you slide back into old behaviors and patterns. After all, if you will only fail, why bother?

As you practice, you begin to develop a track record of success. Relationships improve. You can have difficult conversations with grace and dignity. Your lung capacity and muscle strength increases, and you can run without stopping for thirty minutes. Your debt begins to shrink, and you aren't afraid of the constant creditor calls. Whatever it is you are doing is beginning to work.

You are getting encouragement and insight from your guide and your tribe. When you hit a challenge, they help you explore possible solutions and different behaviors to stay on track. When you stumble and lose some ground, they share how they course-corrected in similar circumstances.

So much has been given to you already by these amazing people. Now it's your turn. Your well is beginning to fill up. But the best way to keep what you have attained is to reach back to the person just a few steps behind you and offer support, the same way it has been offered to you. There is no better way to practice, and solidify your new learning, than to teach someone else what you are beginning to understand.

Like learning a new language, the best way to gain mastery is by daily immersion. You can certainly learn new ideas and skills without practicing them daily, but that's not the route to mastery.

As Malcolm Gladwell says in his landmark work, Outliers (New York: Little Brown, 2008, p. 42): "Practice isn't the thing you do once you're good. It's the thing you do that makes you good."

MAKE ROOM FOR SHIFT

When we commit to practice, and to the time required in order to learn a new behavior, we must make space in our life. If you are like most of us, every minute of every day is accounted for. Sometime more. Where will you find the time or space to start a new way of being? The obvious answer is you will need to make the room by letting something else go.

Where does a new mother find time for her infant? Or a new lover find time for their mate? Where do we find time to learn a new language or move into a new house? We make room by letting other things go. Some shifts are barely noticeable, while others take careful consideration and even the support and assistance of others.

Part of our period of practice is not only recognizing where there are things we need to let go of in our current situation, but paying attention to how we will do so. Equally important is not rushing through this part of shift without expressing gratitude to the things we are either letting go or temporarily setting aside. They served us at one time, even if it was only to buffer us from our fears or traumas.

A ritual of release may even be in order if what you are saying goodbye to has been meaningful to you. At the very least, spend some time meditating on its gifts, and send it some gratitude in farewell.

In this new, cleared space, your fresh practice can really take root, as if you had tilled the soil. Too often we are resentful of the current activities and can't wait to kick them to the curb. When this happens, we unwittingly create an energy of disappointment and resistance, like rocky, uninhabitable soil, which places our new shaky new practice at a serious disadvantage. Let's give it every opportunity to succeed instead.

EXERCISE TO ENHANCE YOUR PRACTICE

1. What is one thing you could do every day to act in alignment with your desires without completely jeopardizing what you are not willing to risk?

   _____

2. Is there another, second, thing you could do?

   _____

3. How about a third thing? Something small but meaningful.

   _____

4. What are you willing to give up to get what you want?

   _____

5. When you hit a stumbling block, what are three things you can do to regain your balance?

   _____

   _____

   _____

6. What is a personal affirmation you can use daily?

   _____

7. How can you activate the support of your guide and your tribe when you are struggling?

   _____

   _____

   _____

CHAPTER NINE

GET UNCOMFORTABLE

THE THING WE HATE MOST is discomfort. When we itch, we immediately want to scratch it. When we are sad or lonely we seek the nearest comfort available, including distraction and addictive behavior. We go to great lengths to suppress the symptoms of the common cold, even though the medications can actually extend the infection itself and even make it worse.

However, there is truth to the statement "no pain, no gain," which is about pushing the boundaries of muscles we have underutilized. The objective is a new state of being that pushes the boundaries of what we thought was possible. The only catch is we tend to want all the benefits of growth without any of the discomfort. That is simply not realistic.

So much has been written about the importance of discomfort for growth. Elizabeth Lombardo, psychologist and author of *Better Than Perfect*, says people who regularly seek out fresh experiences tend to be more creative and emotionally resilient than those who remain stuck in a routine. But these fresh experiences take us out of our comfort zone, and that means we leave our comfort zone—the thing we are inclined to avoid.

Lombardo's stance is that we are stronger and more confident about our personal and professional abilities when we dare to break our own mold. Discomfort, in other words, is a catalyst for growth. It forces you to change, stretch, and adapt.

Research shows that putting yourself in new and unfamiliar situations triggers a unique part of the brain that releases dopamine, that natural happy chemical we discussed in chapter 8. Here's the mind-blower: that unique region of the brain is only activated when you see or experience completely new things. So, to get to the up side of happiness, we must go through the discomfort first. Jack Canfield is quoted as saying, "If we are not a little bit uncomfortable every day, we're not growing. All the good stuff is outside our comfort zone."

The severity of our discomfort at this point depends on how effectively we executed earlier stages and also how deep our limiting beliefs and the obstacles we have experienced are. The harder the shift, then more personal the healing we are undertaking. As many great minds, from Rumi to Ernest Hemingway to Leonard Cohen have said, "We are all broken. That is how the light gets in." Let the light in. Know this is part of the process, and, because you found guidance, you don't have do this alone.

THE REASON FOR OUR PAIN

Our discomfort can be a sign that something is definitely wrong. However, it is also a sign of transformation and rebirth. The art is in knowing the difference, and we often don't. We have spent so much time avoiding discomfort in all its forms.

There is a distinct difference between "good" pain and "bad" pain, which is very important to know at this point in our shift. If we are experiencing "bad" pain—the sort that is a warning that our bodies or our psyche is damaged, we need to immediately move into triage mode.

Similarly, if we are experiencing "good" pain—the sort that comes with the physical birth process, emotional process of shedding of old beliefs, or strengthening our bodies through new activity—then we need to stay on track and surrender to the discomfort so we can learn from it and heal from it.

The physical fitness industry can teach us a lot about the difference between good and bad pain. When it comes to our bodies, there are indicators you're crossing over into serious or "bad" pain. The good pain makes you tired but you keep going. Bad pain comes on all of a sudden, sometimes with a pop, crack, or distinct feeling that something isn't right. That sense that something isn't right is your best clue.

The same can be true in our emotional discomfort.

Although we might feel we can't tell, we are usually able to know the difference between the natural and productive pain of new effort, versus the sharp pain of emotional trauma. When we are trying something a little intimidating, like asking for help or applying for a new job at the risk of rejection, our heart rate speeds up. We might breathe more shallowly. Anxiety and the idea of failing rise up. That's tolerable and reasonable discomfort inherent in transformation.

On the other hand, the sharp, warning pain of an abusive attack or newly discovered traumatic memories that need to be carefully dealt with under therapeutic supervision sends us into fight or flight mode. Often we shut down entirely, or we lash out. Our behaviors can even become hysterical. If you aren't sure which discomfort you are experiencing with this distinction, then approach with caution. Take baby steps. There is no race to the finish line.

Although the common myth is not true that when you help a developing butterfly out of a chrysalis, it grows a swollen body and small, shriveled wings, newly emerged butterflies do have very soft wings and bodies, which haven't hardened yet. Rushing the process by "helping" can kill the creature. Assistance exiting them from their chrysalis is most likely to damage them permanently at the most vulnerable time, which dooms them. Better to allow the natural process, as difficult as it can be, to unfold at the pace nature intended.

RESISTANCE IS FUTILE

The ironic thing about discomfort is that our response makes all the difference. When we resist discomfort—especially feelings like anxiety, sadness, grief, anger, loneliness, and frustration—we focus on it. Our attention to the feeling of discomfort enlarges its place in our awareness. What's more, we tense up and contract. This effort exhausts us, depleting our necessary internal resources for shifting. The Law of Nonresistance states:

Whatever we resist persists.

I encourage my clients, when they express an overwhelming sense of exhaustion in a set of circumstances, to examine where they are resisting. The antidote includes deep breathing, since it is physically impossible to breathe deeply and be anxious at the same time. Additionally, it includes acceptance.

Acceptance is a state of relaxation and full presence with what is happening. It doesn't deny that something is uncomfortable. It simply acknowledges it. Energy and balance are conserved, and the pain lessens in severity.

When I would get vaccinations at the tender age of four or five, my mother would give me a gentle pep talk while the nurse prepped the needle, "Now, remember, relax the muscle in your arm, because it hurts more when you tense up." She was right. Although I would feel the sharp needle, my focus was on relaxing into the pain, which quickly ended, and I barely noticed it. The lollipop and praise for being such a "good girl" was ample reward.

Candidly, it also helped me endure the shot when I knew it was coming. Expecting the sharp pain mentally prepared me. I consciously shifted my focus to remaining relaxed. For this reason alone I am sharing this information about the discomfort you are bound to experience. Relax. Breathe deeply. Focus your attention on staying centered and present. This is only temporary.

DON'T GET DISTRACTED

In our effort to avoid discomfort we tend to look for distractions. These come in all shapes and sizes. Food, alcohol, gambling, relationships, shopping, social media, binging on entertainment, and even activities we generally consider positive, such as work, volunteer service, general "busyness," and even exercise can all be used as a distraction from a deeper emotional disturbance. None of these things are inherently good or bad. It is the level at which we participate in them, and what is not getting our focus as a result, that categorizes them as a distraction or not.

It isn't difficult to tell when something is a distraction (or addiction) rather than a balanced part of your life. The signs will include:

1. A sense of shame or guilt—mild or acute—when you participate

2. An almost irresistible desire to participate, even though there is something else that needs doing that is more in alignment with your priorities

3. A "hangover" effect the next day—feeling exhausted, disoriented, or vaguely dissatisfied at having participated

4. Hiding the behavior

5. Lying about the behavior or minimizing it

6. Planning your life around it

7. A sense of feeling overwhelmed in other areas of your life, where you just can't seem to find all the resources you need

8. Failing to meet other commitments in order to participate

9. Friends and family making direct or indirect comments about the behavior

10. Talking about it all the time, because you think about it all the time

11. Changing who you hang out with because of it

12. Becoming defensive if someone brings it up

13. Wondering if the level at which you participate is healthy or not

14. Getting into legal trouble over it

15. Inability to afford it (but you do it anyway)

Whew! Some of that is intense. Not every distraction lands us in jail, however. Many of our favorite ones receive high social validation when we do them—like working to excess. Again, the answer is a personal, inner one. Look at the list and feel the response inside yourself. You know if something doesn't feel quite right. Is there a behavior on this list you currently could say yes to? Or if not yes, somewhat? Can you say yes to seven or more of these items? That's okay. Don't worry. I am not asking you to do anything about that right now, other than notice. You can hold onto your comfortable distraction. Go ahead and work late. Surf the internet for hours. It feels safer and certainly less uncomfortable sometimes. I get it.

What I ask you to do, however, is to elevate your awareness around whatever your distraction might be. How are you feeling when you get the urge to engage with it? What is it that you don't get to do as a result? How do you feel immediately as a result of the activity? Those are actually the most likely reasons for the behavior in the first place.

If you are able to stop what you are currently distracting yourself with, even for a day, observe the feelings that come up. They won't be wonderful, but it's just one day. Remember the needle. Relax. It will be over soon. You can return to your distraction shortly if you must. However, this distraction is quite likely to be one of the root obstacles in your transformation. So sooner or later you will be led to let it go.

It might be harder than you think at first. Alcoholics are famous for protesting: I can quit any time I choose to! (But they can't.) And for those of us who blame their weak willpower, you might want to turn the mirror on yourself first, for a little bit of understanding. We all have distractions in our lives. Just some of us have them at greater levels than others.

Most of our addiction is in our mind—true. But the mind is a big place, as we have discussed—full of the subconscious, the ego, fears, beliefs, feelings, emotions—and all of it gets twisted up together sometimes. The rest is in the dopamine hit you get from it.

That was the case with me and my "shopping habit." I had a substantial income and high stress environment with my agency, and shopping was a great stress reliever, giving me a nice dopamine hit every time something new arrived. Of course, when my income dropped off dramatically the first year I was back in business for myself, I did not adjust my shopping pattern.

My income had, for a time, masked my distraction. To be quite candid, by then, it was an addiction. My husband commented on it. So I had stuff shipped to my office where he wouldn't see it arrive. My co-workers commented on the daily shipments, and I laughed it off. Friends said things like, "You never wear the same outfit twice!" And the UPS deliveryman knew me by name, saying, "It looks like the money never runs out." When the money did run out, my credit card balances started to climb.

Intellectually, I realized that it needed to stop. I knew it wasn't fair to my husband, and the spending jeopardized our financial well-being. And yet, when the catalog or the email arrived, I had to have a look. There was always something I simply had to have. This inner conflict is the hallmark of the battle inside every addict battling with their addiction. Knowing something is wrong is not enough to offset the seduction of good feeling, however temporary, the addiction provides.

Fortunately for me, COVID-19 happened. The world came to a stop. My husband's salary was so severely reduced that we had to cut our living expenses in half. But something else happened too: the stress level plummeted. I was working out on my back deck for hours, with the birds singing and the sun delivering a ton of good old vitamin D. Reasons to go out and run an errand (always a dangerous activity for a shopper) evaporated. We made dinners at home, watched movies together, and I re-amplified my writing, which fulfilled a creative need I had been ignoring.

When I stopped shopping, my sense of shame and guilt lifted. I quite literally got two or three extra hours back in my day. I felt calmer, happier, and more fulfilled in a way the shopping couldn't begin to offer me. As a result, my habit of distraction was broken. Could I go back to it? I'm certain I could in a heartbeat if I chose to go down that path.

The key in breaking free from any distraction is to interrupt the behavior long enough to substitute a fresh, healthier behavior. This will mean facing the fear associated with losing the distraction our addiction provided, and freeing ourselves from its grip.

EXERCISE TO REVEAL YOUR DISCOMFORT

To find the places where you are most tender, in need of healing, look to the places you are distracting yourself from your own emotional discomfort. Let's use the list of signs of distracting behaviors from this chapter. You will recognize some of the following list in one area of your life (for example, work) while others show up in other areas (for example, your health). See how many of these apply for you:

1. A sense of shame or guilt—mild or acute—when you participate in a behavior

2. An almost irresistible desire to participate, even though there is something else that needs doing that is more in alignment with your priorities

3. A "hangover" effect the next day—feeling exhausted, disoriented, or vaguely dissatisfied at having participated in a behavior

4. Hiding the behavior

5. Lying about the behavior or minimizing it

6. Planning your life around it

7. A sense of feeling overwhelmed in other areas of your life, where you just can't seem to find all the resources you need

8. Failing to meet other commitments in order to participate

9. Friends and family making direct or indirect comments about the behavior

10. Talking about it all the time, because you think about it all the time

11. Changing who you hang out with because of it

12. Becoming defensive if someone brings it up

13. Wondering if the level you participate is healthy or not

14. Getting into legal trouble over it

15. Inability to afford it, but you do it anyway

For each item you checked as a applying to you, write down what area of your life is affected and what situations or feelings trigger you to distract yourself. Now, instead of trying to force yourself to behave differently, when you notice yourself picking up your distraction/addiction each time, simultaneously pay attention to the feelings you are avoiding through the behavior, and send yourself the energy of love and acceptance.

Say this phrase to yourself as often as you need to throughout the day until you begin to feel the discomfort dissipate:

"Even though I (describe feeling here) whenever (describe situation here), I completely love and accept myself."

This is the foundational statement in tapping—also known as Emotional Freedom Technique (EFT)—and can be reinforced with the kinesthetic memory used in tapping. If you want to amplify this practice, there are many videos and books available on the subject.

CHAPTER TEN

BE THE OUTCOME

ACHIEVING YOUR SHIFT can take infinite possible paths. Some paths you choose, and some are chosen for you. How you show up—with openness, adaptability, intention, willingness, and even curiosity and wonder—will have a measurable impact on the shift you are manifesting right now. There is a co-creation happening between you and the universe. As much as you may feel you are ready to shift your outer experience immediately, there is an inner shift that must happen first. You are not just changing your life—you are changing yourself right now.

Whatever shift you are undertaking is okay. You might want to have a bigger house, greater income, a soul mate, a better body, or a new career. Or you may not want things at all. Instead you might want to be of greater service, have deeper friendships, be more creative, happier, more fulfilled, or feel at peace in your life. All of those are equally "good."

There is a well-known approach to getting what we desire, which is the focus of the popular book *The Secret*. It encourages us to ask for what we want, because the universe will only say "Yes" to our requests. Unfortunately, that's only part of the story. If it were this simple, anyone could win the lottery, and no one we love would ever pass away. There is a lot more to realizing our desires than wanting them and asking for them.

The practice of affirmative prayer is a prayer of knowing, instead of a prayer of pleading or supplication. It is best described in the New Testament. In Mark 11:24 (ESV), Jesus teaches us to pray this way: "whatever you ask in prayer, believe that you have received it, and it will be yours." In fact, the common ending to many prayers, "Amen," means "so be it."

Still, if we consider his guidance at face value, something doesn't seem quite right. If I pray for my loved one who is experiencing end of life decline, will I make them immortal through my prayers? Of course not! So, is it possible for both Jesus' statement, and the natural law of the cycle of life to both be true? Yes.

FOLLOW THE FEELING

Our true desires spring from a place in us that is beyond words. In this inner sanctum, marketers and our mothers have no influence over us. We want our shift for our own reasons. We want those things that move us in the inevitable direction of our evolving purpose. While purpose sounds lofty and beyond any desire for "stuff," it's possible that the next stage of our growth might actually include a new body, house, career, or lover. Material desires are natural and empowering when they are serving a higher purpose and the focus is on something even greater.

If you accept that you are more than your physical body, and this world has meaning beyond our physical experience, then you can accept that this shift you are undertaking is actually a spiritual activity—a dance with mystical influences. If you believe in God, that may be easy for you to embrace. If, however, you do not, then lean into the laws of quantum physics and the unpredictability of the invisible realms of energy, where particles behave differently based on how the observer is viewing them.

Either way, your shift is a movement of energy and attention, both inside and outside yourself. If you try to shift through mental and physical means alone, you will burn out very quickly. It will be as if you were running across the hot coals and embers of the fire. The way to shift faster, and with less effort, is to hold a vision of yourself as if the shift had already occurred.

Ask yourself: what will shift look like, and feel like, on the other side? Imagine yourself transformed. Be vivid in your vision. Consider how you will look, whom you will hang out with, where you will live, and how you will spend your time. Once you have a good idea about your dream goals, begin to act as if you are already there. If you are going to keep company with particular people, start connecting with them through groups, associations, or communities where they are. If you would live in a certain place, then visit it. The more you familiarize yourself with the end result, the more you identify with it, and the more easily you become it.

Vision boards are very popular right now for manifesting desires. They really can be an awesome tool. However, they operate on a limited plane as well. To really embody what a shift would feel like it is extremely helpful to engage all your senses—visual, auditory, olfactory, tactile—and do everything in your power to be the change you are seeking, even in advance of it being a fact.

Our imagination is fertile ground for this exercise. We can perform daily visualization meditations. Or we can associate our activities and personal connections with those who already are where we want to be. I had been telling myself since I was fourteen that I would "go to Peru someday." I was challenged to do some visualizing work to bring that dream to life. I grabbed a photo of Machu Picchu off the internet and Photoshopped myself into it, then printed it out. I began studying Spanish and reading about the history of the region.

I knew two people who had been to Peru recently, and so I bought them coffee to pick their brains about what they recommended doing and seeing there. The second person shared that he was leading a group to Peru in just a couple of months—did I want to join? Because it was a group, with someone whom I knew and trusted, the uncertainty and cost barriers were removed in an instant—enough so that my husband could also afford to go with me too!

For ten days we traveled with two shamans, were able to visit ruins that were typically not open to the public, wandered through gardens filled with hummingbirds and wildflowers, and hiked to the Sun Gate atop Machu Picchu. It was, perhaps, the trip of a lifetime for me. All this happened in just weeks, because I let myself act as if I were going, before I knew I was going.

The same is true for my weight loss journey. My entire adult life I had been trying to "lose a few pounds." Over thirty years those "few pounds" went from five to fifty—while I was trying to lose them! I tried every diet fad intermittently and wreaked havoc with my metabolism in the process. I exercised off and on, got a trainer a couple of times briefly, and still the weight kept creeping up as I traveled, got little sleep, ate out regularly, ate sugary treats and drank empty alcohol calories in between my efforts to lose.

At last I have recognized that if I wanted to be healthy, I have to embody the behaviors and habits of a healthy person. Now I jog for thirty minutes six or seven days a week, avoid sugar and alcohol except for celebrations, get eight or nine hours of rest, and eat mostly whole foods with a focus on fruits and vegetables. I study exercises and try new ones for strength. I explore various kinds of yoga, and I walk in my beautiful neighborhood on the river. I clip healthy recipes and study wellness like I used to study the dessert menu.

It is likely no surprise that every day I lose an ounce or two, and I am not racing an invisible clock. Now this is who I see myself as—a healthy person, becoming even healthier, rather than an unhealthy person trying to get healthy.

While these two shifts might seem too simplistic for you, for me they were nothing of the sort. That's the fascinating thing about difficult shifts—what is hard for us can be a no-brainer for someone else. This is because they are our shift! It bears repeating: the harder the shift is for us, the more necessary it is for our soul's evolution.

Shifting becomes real and sustainable when we see ourselves differently, from the inside out. Instead of waiting for the shift to occur so we can change, we change so the shift can occur. The only way that can happen is by embodying the shift even in its apparent absence.

STAY IN THE MOMENT

However eager we might be to shift, we can still hold our goal at arms length in an undefined future time. This is a trap for us for two very important reasons. The first is that when we assert that we do not yet have the object of our desire, we are not practicing the mindset or behaviors that will maintain it later. When someone defers their happiness and freedom until they retire, for example, research shows that they have no practice with happiness and freedom, and, as a result retirement fails to fulfill its promise for them.

The second is that where we focus, we flourish. If we focus on what we don't yet have, it just holds our current lack firmly in place. We are actually focusing on the lack we are experiencing right now. When we don't view ourselves actively being the person who has already shifted, we inevitably see ourselves as the person who has not. That, then, is exactly who we remain.

The only time that shift can happen is now. ***Shift isn't the outcome***. It is the process of becoming. So, even though you have no tangible results in your hands right in this moment, you can take action towards it, and, in my experience, it will move towards you in return. In the meanwhile, if it is love you are longing for, be more loving—especially to yourself. If it is financial prosperity, then relish whatever pennies you now have—you know, the ones in the sofa cushion, and the free concert in the park. If you know you need to be doing different work, then do your current work with greater passion and continue to explore what else is possible. If you wish you were happier, then do the things that bring you joy and spend time in the company of others who are happy.

We can become so focused on what is missing that we miss the opportunities to claim what is right in front of us! However, when we are fully present in this moment, our awareness is amplified, our senses are heightened, and we are no longer afraid of our discomfort or afraid of our old limiting beliefs. We become part of something much greater than ourselves, and shift is the natural result.

VISUALIZATION EXERCISE:
PERMISSION TO DREAM

Daydreaming is a natural gift we all have as children. As we grow up and become more socialized we often dismiss the activity as a waste of time without any redeeming merits. This is actually one of the most pervasive myths in our culture. When we allow ourselves to see something with our mind's eye in vivid detail, we alter our own energy and bodily functions. Our bodies don't know the difference between material reality and imagination—and that can work to our advantage!

When you strongly desire a fresh shift in your life, use creative visualization to accelerate reaching your goal. Visualization was taught by Jesus ("Ask all these things knowing they are already given to you...") and Cicero, written about in *The Canterbury Tales*, expanded upon by Neville Goddard in *The Power of Imagination*, popularized by New Thought writers like Shakti Gawain, and explored in experimental psychology. Creative visualization is a well-accepted method of rewiring our brain.

Here is the easy creative visualization approach:

Stage 1: Image Generation. Relax. Close you eyes and go into a light meditative state. Imagine yourself in the presence of the object of your desire. See it in great detail.

Stage 2: Image Maintenance. As this implies, maintain your inner view of your desire. You must hold your focus for a period of time—which could be just a few minutes, or as long as you like. You are simply observing.

Stage 3: Image Inspection. As you are holding your image in your focus, begin to inspect it and explore it, elaborating on the image in detail, and embellish on the experience—for example, if you attain the desire, what will you say? Who would be with you? What would you look like? How would you dress? What would others say about you? Where would you live? The list is endless.

Stage 4: Image Transformation. Focus on the feelings of having your desire fulfilled. How will you feel differently? Immerse yourself in the positive emotions, feeling them in the visualization itself.

When you have completed all four stages, scan yourself. If you feel complete, you may set the visualization process aside. If not, you can repeat the process from the beginning. Once you feel complete, simply say to yourself: This or something better is mine. And so it is.

CHAPTER ELEVEN

CHOOSE YOU

THE GREATEST OBSTACLE to our own shift is our self. We are inclined to negative thinking, with our inner dialog being 80 percent negative self-talk. This is enough to dampen the first spark of our shift. It is compounded when we share our shift with others who are jealous or unsupportive. Your guide should be a cheerleader for you—even so, you must still be your greatest cheerleader by far. You must choose you. Doing so will set yourself on fire to achieve the shift you desire.

A few decades ago, Japanese scientist and author Masaru Emoto demonstrated that human consciousness has a remarkable physical effect on the molecular structure of water. In Japan, he discovered that water in the large city where he lived, when frozen, formed shapeless, muddy crystals. He then found that water from up in the mountains, when frozen, formed beautiful, snowflake-like crystals. Initially he believed the different crystal formations might be due to pollution.

However, as his studies evolved, he found that the shapeless crystal water from the city could be altered to form beautiful crystals, and the mountain stream water formed shapeless crystals under certain circumstances.

His experiments altered the harmony and balance of water crystal formation by using positive and negative words directed at the water! He found that when he and his students spoke positive words over the water, like love, or positively imbued names like Mother Teresa, when the water was frozen, it formed beautiful, balanced, and harmonious crystals. And when they spoke negative words like hate, or even names like Hitler, the frozen water produced amorphous and muddy crystals.

Now—whatever you think of these experiments (and there are a lot of opinions about them)—know that our thoughts and our bodies, as well as the water itself, are all energy at a molecular level. Additionally, our bodies are approximately 60 percent water.

Since our brains are inclined towards negativity, this is particularly important. Research shows we each have between twelve thousand to sixty thousand thoughts every day, and as many as 98 percent of them are repetitive. Even more significantly, 80 percent of those same thoughts are negative. Not to be a Debbie Downer—but additional studies indicate that it takes no less than three positive thoughts to neutralize just one negative thought.

In my group presentations I call up a volunteer from the audience. I have them hold out their arms at shoulder height, and I apply pressure at their wrists, asking them to resist. The pressure is nominal, and they have no problem. Then I say the word "love." They are able to maintain their arm position again, with no issue. Lastly, I offer them the word "hate." As you can gather, at that point their arms drop about three to four inches when I apply pressure. Everyone gasps—as does the volunteer. Afterwards I also ask the audience to collectively speak the word "love" three times in unison, which restores the volunteer's energy and balance.

This startling kinesthetic demonstration shows how our negative self-talk—or the negative talk we receive from those around us—has a direct impact on our physical strength as well as our motivation. Especially when it is just below the level of our awareness. Applying positive thinking, or a few affirmations here and there, won't overcome this additive effect.

What does work is to practice loving and accepting ourselves exactly as we are, where we are, unconditionally. I have read and listened to teachers, coaches, and motivators who suggest that we will be more likely to make meaningful change by imagining how sad or disappointed our friends and families will be if we fail. Others suggest we should tell people about our plans so we know they will be judging us on how we do. These individuals are proponents of negative motivation theory. Like them, many of us subscribe to negative motivation via our own inner dialogue. We are, as they say, our own worst critic.

Although there are those who would disagree with me, I believe that negative motivation actually deters us from making the really important shifts. According to David Burns in *Feeling Good: The New Mood Therapy Revised and Updated* (New York: HarperCollins, 1999), there are thirteen ways we sabotage ourselves with negative motivation:

1. Hopelessness
2. Helplessness
3. Overwhelming yourself
4. Jumping to conclusions

5. Self-labeling
6. Undervaluing the Rewards
7. Perfectionism
8. Fear of failure
9. Fear of success
10. Fear of disapproval or criticism
11. Coercion and resentment
12. Low frustration tolerance
13. Guilt and self-blame

While we may find the rewards we dangle in front of ourselves and others still do not generate the action we believe they ought to, I am suggesting the rewards are not the issue. On the contrary, positive motivation doesn't work because we either don't really want what is on offer, or we are afraid. If we are afraid, it is fear that something is either not possible or is ultimately less desirable than our current situation. Negative motivation only makes us feel worse. If any of the negative motivations I listed sound like something you may be creating for yourself, I encourage you to drop them as quickly as possible. If they worked, you wouldn't be here with me now.

The best motivator in the world is hope. It has built religions, countries, and companies; altered societies; created new technologies; landed us in outer space; and discovered incredible inner spaces as well.

The second-best motivator is gratitude. A recognition of our successes, our gifts, our blessings of all sizes, and our greater potential actually gives us hope. When I can be grateful precisely where I am, my energy to keep going is amplified. I skew my perspective towards the good, not the bad, of my existence, and am more likely, as a result, to create more good going forward.

The third best motivator is curiosity. It challenges us to think outside the box we, and our society, can become trapped in. Curiosity pushes us in positive and creative ways. It is the foundation for new learning, which is why we need it so dearly as children and must never lose it as adults.

The fourth best motivator is compassion, especially for ourselves. When we can become compassionate with ourselves at times when we fall short of our expectations, we can see more clearly why we did so. If we become entangled in judging and criticizing our shortcomings, we also become stuck in them. Compassion provides a clearer perspective—and makes us curious about how we can try a different way.

The fifth motivator is acceptance. This does not mean accepting the unacceptable, but rather seeing things as they really are. Most importantly, acceptance respects and trusts our process, fears, desires, and gifts without judgment or shame. It has discernment of exactly where we are, and it allows us the time and lessons we need to move forward.

Lastly, the foundational motivator is awareness itself. For us to have motivation at all we must know what we want and who we are becoming. This is the very essence of life itself. Life is creation, and if ever there was a self-motivating entity, it would be life.

Infuse your journey with hope, gratitude, curiosity, compassion, acceptance, and awareness. You will be amazed at the difference. You will catch fire.

EXERCISE: CHECK YOUR MOTIVATION

When you are feeling a lack of motivation, return here, to this chapter. Remember Burns's list of negative motivators.

Check in with yourself and see if you are unintentionally using any. Then, replace your inner dialogue by activating the true, positive motivators.

Negative Motivators:

1. Hopelessness
2. Helplessness
3. Overwhelming yourself
4. Jumping to conclusions
5. Self-labeling
6. Undervaluing the rewards
7. Perfectionism
8. Fear of failure
9. Fear of success
10. Fear of disapproval or criticism
11. Coercion and resentment
12. Low frustration tolerance
13. Guilt and self-blame

Positive Motivators:

1. Hope
2. Gratitude
3. Curiosity
4. Compassion
5. Acceptance
6. Awareness/Consciousness

CHAPTER TWELVE

CELEBRATE THE SHIFT

PERFECTION IS JUST AN IDEA. Too often we become slaves to whatever we have chosen to call perfection. Enslavement to perfection means we will not allow ourselves to live fully or be free of our burdens. The heaviest burden of them all is the belief that there is a finish line and an end to our personal evolution. There is a phrase that reveals our enslavement: "If only [object or situation of our desires] was true, then I could be okay."

We defer any joy (or being entirely "okay") from the accomplishments we have already created, until every single aspect of our shift aligns perfectly. We have all heard the saying "Progress, not perfection." Still, although we embrace the idea intellectually, we continue to beat ourselves up or drive ourselves forward towards that elusive ideal of perfection we are holding ourselves to.

There is absolutely nothing more important in shift than celebrating every win along the way. Failure to do so is demoralizing and keeps us stuck. When we celebrate our wins, it generates enthusiasm for the next stage, and so on. In truth, no shift is final. Each shift leads to the next, and the next, whether we are able to see what is around the corner or not. This is how we grow—one stage, and one micro shift at a time. When we see our progress in this evolutionary perspective, we can relax into the journey and, for the most part, enjoy the ride.

CONFESSIONS OF AN OVERACHIEVER

For decades I have often been complimented for being "driven." Many people have asked me how I manage to accomplish so much. There was a time I loved hearing that, and it made me proud. Today I recognize that being driven can be as much of an obstacle as it is a benefit. It certainly brought me a lot of money, recognition, and approval, but it also exhausted me, damaged my health, and robbed me of my joy just as often.

For each persona we embody, there is a counterpart, called the shadow self. If the counterpart is suppressed or repressed, areas of our life will have imbalances. The shadow self of my driven persona, the Overachiever, is the Carefree Child. I remember the exact moment, when I was four years old, that I decided to be productive and busy.

It was a bright, summer morning, and my father was busy doing some work around the house. He was very intent on his work, going in and out with tools in hand. I have no idea what particular project had his focus, but I remember how attracted I was to his energy. I began following his every step. I was curious and playful—bouncing along, asking him what he was doing.

He did not share my enthusiasm. He was intent on fixing something, and his four-year-old daughter was dogging his every move. At one point he stopped in frustration and turned sharply, so I almost ran into him. He said loudly, "Are you bored? You have lots of toys. You need to go find something else to do and stop following me! There is never an excuse to be bored."

In actuality, I hadn't been bored at all. But staring at my father, who was obviously very irritated with me, I made a decision that moment to push aside that wonder and curiosity, following Daddy around. Never be bored, he had said. And I never was again. I was productive. I was useful. That decision was mine. My father never intended for me to divorce a part of me that morning. Yet I did. The Carefree Child was suppressed.

What did that sweet little girl want? Just to observe and be in her father's presence. But she was in the way, taking up too much space. She was an irritant and a bother, worthy only of rejection. Or, more precisely, that's what she heard. From then on, I slammed a lid on her, closed her away, and only let her come out to play on rare occasions. She was blocking me from my father's love and approval, after all.

Of course, when we divorce from a part of us, we create an imbalance. When we choose to judge part of ourselves as bad or wrong, we demonize our wholeness. Referred to as a "shadow self" in some healing practices, this exiled piece of us begins to act out in order to regain its rightful place. This shows up in being triggered by situations, or, as with me, imbalanced aspects of our lives.

That playful, curious little girl has always deserved to be a full part of me. I asked her what she wants now—what would let her feel seen. I asked how could I reassure her that she matters to me. Her answer was poignant and precious:

"Stacey—I want to come out and play. I don't want to be so serious and goal-oriented. Can we just chase some fireflies, watch the rain, and jump in a puddle? Can we lie down on the ground and look up at the trees, listening to the birds? Can we climb that hill, just because it's there?"

Of course, you can, honey. I'll join you. How could anyone not feel an overflowing of love for you?

And I set aside my list, turned off my notifications, put my phone on silent. And we went for a walk in the woods.

That's progress.

I continue to learn the many origins of my ideas about how good it is to be busy, productive, and useful. There are many more besides that pivotal moment with my father—from experiences with teachers to those with bosses, friends, peers, and clients.

Our culture is quite addicted to the idea of productivity's primary importance. When I accomplish something, I get that endorphin hit of approval. When that happens, my little girl can shrink a bit back into her shadowy corner. I forget she is there. I forget that I promised she would matter to me. Trust is broken.

I am on a journey of unlearning the lessons that eroded my wholeness and my balance. The four-year-old Stacey, full of playful curiosity, is not the only piece of me I shut off. Many parts of me are waiting for me to go on a search-and-rescue mission and bring them back to myself.

It's a tricky business, because I can just as easily shut off productive, useful Stacey as playful Stacey. Neither one is bad or wrong. Instead, my shift is about integrating the two for greater balance. There is always room for more of me.

Because I am a recovering overachiever, I am well qualified to address the innate desire to not stop—and not rest—until perfection has been achieved.

After all, isn't that the whole point?

No. It is not.

The point is to be in appreciation for the wonder of it all. The minute I slip into judgment and criticism of any part of me, I am severing myself from something I need in order to evolve. That is an idea my overachiever self struggles with, but I let her struggle and love her through it. I celebrate that she got me this far, and I do the same with every other aspect of myself I am getting to meet along the way.

OH, MY PAWS AND WHISKERS! I'M LATE! I'M LATE!

The only perfect time is now. The White Rabbit seemed to be in such a hurry in that children's classic, *Alice in Wonderland*. Our journey can feel that way as well. But when you dig into the symbolism of our friend the rabbit, he is actually the spark of curiosity that activates Alice's spiritual awakening—like an alarm bell going off. It is the White Rabbit who leads Alice down the rabbit hole, and he is the objective Alice runs after and searches for endlessly in Wonderland, a symbol of her quest for knowledge. The White Rabbit showed up at precisely the right time, not a minute too soon or too late.

Once we begin to see the results of our shift, it can be tempting to feel regret that we did not make changes sooner. We wonder why we stayed in the job or the marriage, let our weight creep up so far, or never got around to having children.

The implication is that we failed to act in a timely or appropriate way. Again, that insidious voice of judgment creeps in. It is telling us we were wrong, misguided, or—worse—stupid. That is the voice of the wounded ego fighting for its life.

Instead, try a healthy dose of appreciation, since this moment is the one we are living in, and no other.

A RAMPAGE OF APPRECIATION

One of the greatest forms of celebration is appreciation. Akin to gratitude, it allows us not only to savor the experience we are having right now—like a gorgeous sunset—but also to notice the experiences that brought us here. That latter appreciation can be a little difficult for some experiences, especially if they included something traumatic, as many of us can claim.

It is easy for me to suggest that you appreciate the abuse you suffered, because it "made you who you are today." But if you aren't exactly in love with who you are, and you haven't yet moved into a space of forgiveness or done the deep healing work, that will not only fall flat, it will sound slightly obscene. So don't force the appreciation if you are not there yet. Forcing it is not only unhelpful, it can actually be harmful. Just be aware that you are not there yet, and keep reading. As you understand the process, again, you can take micro-shifts to your own healing.

Appreciation is crucial, since it anchors our awareness of what is working for us today—even if it is only that we didn't eat the entire cream-cheese covered cupcake, or that we actually got out of bed today. If we can appreciate the micro-shifts, we pave the way for the macro-shift we are undertaking.

The question then is, what can you appreciate without feeling disingenuous, or worse, like a traitor to your experience? I found the best place to begin incorporating appreciation into my experience is with an amazing activity first described by Esther and Jerry Hicks in their book about the teaching of Abraham, *Ask and It Is Given,* called a Rampage of Appreciation.

We can all find something to be grateful for, as we often hear suggested in gratitude list exercises. These are great, but we do tend to keep our appreciation at a shallow level, repeating the same four or five things, day in and day out. That limits our ability to grow in gratitude, and we will quickly tire of the exercise if we stay there.

I have had clients in early stages of shift tell me vehemently that they couldn't think of anything to be grateful for. Others complained that coming up with daily gratitudes felt like an awful chore! This is a result of either being out of practice with the habits of appreciation and gratitude or of overthinking the entire process.

A Rampage of Appreciation, by definition, means to rush headlong into expressing gratitude and appreciation. This wild approach shakes us out of our inertia and can actually create a gratitude high. It removes our tendency to overthink, moving our awareness into that heart space where intuition lives.

Here's how it is done:

Take a moment to center yourself; close your eyes if it is safe. Take a deep breath or two, then open your eyes, and, whatever they land on, begin. Whether your eyes land on the window, the dog, a speck of dust, or a tree outside, speak your gratitude for it: "I am so grateful for this speck of dust!" Then, without thinking, or pausing to reflect, connect that gratitude to another, like this: "I am so grateful for the table the dust is on!" and continue this process for several minutes (at least three): "I am so grateful for the wood the table is made from. I am grateful for the tree that provided the wood—probably from North Carolina. I am grateful for the hands and tools that made the table. I am grateful that the table fits so perfectly in my room. I am grateful that I found the table in the store. I am grateful that the store was there when I was looking for a table. I am grateful for the family that owns the store. I am grateful to be able to afford this furniture. I am grateful I have a job right now..."

A whole new mindset arises from a speck of dust. And isn't that what shift is all about? Never dismiss the power of a speck of dust. Appreciate it. You may be amazed by what you will discover. And appreciate every spec of shift you have already begun.

THIS IS YOUR SHIFT

So here we are, at the end of your new beginning. I celebrate how far we have come together. As with most self-help books, the ideas contained here are only as good as the use you put them to and the practice you create for yourself as a result. Otherwise, this book will find a spot in the back of your bookshelf, and you will vaguely remember something about shifting in a couple of years, as you hand it off to Goodwill. Let's not make this one of those cast-off, half-hearted attempts.

Successful—unstoppable—transformation isn't a result of spontaneous combustion. You must set yourself on fire.

ABOUT THE AUTHOR

Stacey is a leadership coach, minister, and has been a successful entrepreneur for over three decades. As an acclaimed marketer, Stacey was named one of the Top 50 Entrepreneurs in Atlanta in her 30's, twice awarded the Top 100 "It" Agencies by Experiential Marketer Magazine, and built two multi-million dollar agencies.

She also understands the unique challenge and discomfort of making the hard transformations life demands of us all. She has struggled with two failed marriages, experienced debilitating impostor syndrome, overwhelm, exhaustion and disillusionment. It took a personal crisis to shatter her limited beliefs about what real success looked like.

Her journey through all these challenges inspired her to work with others who are on fire to have their own breakthrough transformations. She is a Certified Professional Coach, as well as Certified Belief Clearing Practitioner.

SUGGESTED BOOK CLUB QUESTIONS

1. What is the central idea discussed in the book? What personal transformational challenges does the author explore?

2. Do the issues affect your life? How so—directly on a daily basis, or more generally? Now or sometime in the future?

3. What evidence does the author use to support the book's ideas? Is the evidence convincing...definitive or...speculative? Does the author depend on personal opinion, observation, and assessment? Or is the evidence factual—based on science, statistics, historical documents, or quotations from (credible) experts?

4. What are the biggest challenges we all face during personal transformation that can block us?

5. What solutions does the author propose? Are the author's recommendations concrete, sensible, doable? Who would implement those solutions?

6. How controversial are the ideas raised in the book? Did any of them upset you?

7. Talk about specific passages that struck you as significant— or interesting, profound, amusing, illuminating, disturbing, sad...? What was memorable?

8. What have you learned after reading this book? Has it broadened your perspective about a difficult transformation you have dealt with (or are dealing with)?

9. Did the author's personal stories and examples help you see yourself in a clearer light? Or did they seem too unique for identification?

10. Are there any exercises in the book that particularly resonated with you and provided a deeper understanding of yourself?

Book Club Questions courtesy of *LitLovers*

Made in USA - Crawfordsville, IN
68085_9780999515631
01.19.2021 0622